PARALLELS

Diana Cockrill

authorHOUSE®

AuthorHouse™ UK Ltd.
500 Avebury Boulevard
Central Milton Keynes, MK9 2BE
www.authorhouse.co.uk
Phone: 08001974150

First published by AuthorHouse   9/29/2010

ISBN: 978-1-4520-8113-7 (sc)

This book is printed on acid-free paper.

"He that undertaketh the story of a time, especially of any length, cannot but meet with many blanks and spaces which he must be forced to fill up out of his own wit and conjecture."

Francis Bacon, *Advancement of Learning*, 1605

TO MY GRANDSONS

JAKE AND RYAN MONK

who may wish to know something

about their ancestry

ACKNOWLEDGEMENTS

My story has a great many roots. . Most of the people mentioned in it were related to me in some way. It could not have been written had my father not been a good teller of tales and my mother a scribbler. He was not above telling the same story to several different people, altering one or two things to suit his audience, and I have been very surprised to find in one or two publications tales which he also told me when we sat in front of the study fire on a winter evening. But errors and inadequacies must be mine alone, and not attributed to any other source, whether printed or verbal.

Some books came from my father's shelves. They are mostly out of print but for their background information and in one case a photograph, I acknowledge them here:

Astbury, A.K.   The Black Fens: S R Publishers Limited, Cambridge 1958
HMSO   Harvest Home, London 1948
Rotary Club of Ely, 1947 Battle of the Banks, Ely 1948
Stevens, Beatrice   Stretham, a Feast of Memories: Providence Press 1989
                         Edgar – an unpublished memoir
Stretham Parish Council Stretham, the Millennium History:
                         Cambridge Heritage Associates Ltd. 2000
Wentworth Day, James   History of the Fens:
                         George Harrap & Co. Ltd. London, 1954

Other publications in which my father's tales appeared are:
Fire and Steam/Mishaps involving Fenland Pumping Engines
                Stretham Engine Preservation Trust, 1995

Article in Cambs, Hunts & Peterborough Life, July 1972

I hope that those I have mentioned, or their living descendants, will accept that I have dealt fairly with them, and it remains only to apologise to all those organisations and people who have not been specifically named.

PREFACE

This book does not set out to be any kind of official history. It begins, and ends, in my own imagination, although the events I describe are historically correct. It is more a general portrait of two parallels, the life of my mother and myself, expanded to include various other relations. My mother and I were both born at, and raised next door to, fen beam engines, in her case the Hundred Foot and in mine, Stretham. We were both daughters of Drainage Superintendents, both went to what were even in my day fairly primitive village schools and both in our day attended The High School in Ely. That is one parallel. The other is the two great rivers, the Old Bedford and the New Bedford, which simplified, and yet complicated, the drainage of the Fens.

Before we begin with a story, we need a map.

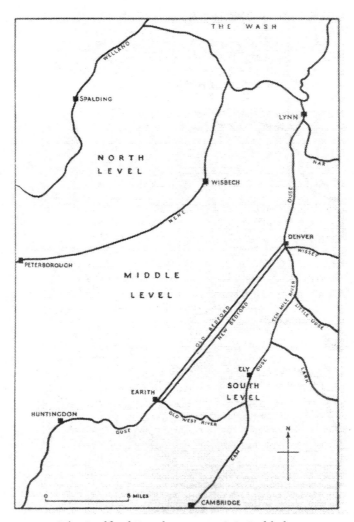

The Bedford Level: courtesy S R Publishers

THE DRAINING OF THE FENS

"Cornelius, je bint een dagdromer!" He had lived in England for many years but still had the entire expatriate's determination not to be swallowed up by an adopted country. So he spoke, and thought, in Dutch, his native language. Now he made a little grimace, a wriggle of his lips, something he did when annoyed either with himself or other people. He must take this new idea, this day-dream, to his patron, the Earl of Bedford, who in turn would have to take it to the Lord Protector, Oliver Cromwell, who would no doubt find some good reason why the necessary capital should be withheld yet again. He sighed. The world of politics and the real world so often failed to co-operate. Thus it had always been, and he supposed it would always be the same. When he was introduced to Cromwell as the Earl's protégé, he remembered the rasping voice saying, "Mijnheer Vermuyden, you have already drained Hatfield Chase so that my Lord here can hunt more successfully. That caused local jealousy and led to rioting. You know that they swore they would man the banks with loaded guns until the whole Level was drowned again, and you and your foreign labourers could swim home like ducks. Now you wish to drain the Fens. I have enough trouble in this pestiferous country, without you causing more destruction. I know these Fen-men. They will not want the land drained, they will want to go on poaching wildfowl and fish, and they will rise up and destroy any works that you make. They will level your houses and break down your banks. You have your knighthood – be content with that! I tell you, reducing the Fens to summer wetland is all that your Adventurers can hope for." So the river, the Bedford River in honour of the Earls of Bedford, had been dug to achieve this, cutting a sharp slash from Denver where the tidal water petered out to Earith and it joined with the original course of the Ouse, reversing the flow of the latter. "Oooze," he said to himself, giving it the full benefit of long Dutch vowels and shaking his head.

That was the trouble. That was why he was standing looking across that newly dug river just the other side of Denver, trying to rationalise what he'd seen in his mind's eye, like a vision sent from God. Ooze, sediment, silt, dropped by the tides that came in from The Wash and the North Sea, blocking up the Bedford River as fast as teams of labourers could dig it free. The Ouse had a gradient of no more than one inch in a mile and a very shallow scour. So the up tide left its burden but the ebb tide didn't take the load away unless there was heavy inland rainfall when some of it would be shifted back out to sea. And he, Cornelius Vermuyden, had the job of sorting it all out.

"There must be sluices. Here – at this village. What do they call it – yes, Denver. They must bar the way to this silt-bearing water." Then again he made the little face, shook his head. "No. We build sluices, like in Holland, but here if the tide is high and the inland water high we have floods again, and so back to where we started. Cornelius, what you first saw was the answer, but I do not think the Earl will like what you say, even though they speak of making him a Duke."

1

It might have been the light, which across that watery flat plain of the fen country intensified everything, just as it did in Holland. Something, in the time it took to blink, to gaze across towards Little Downham and, shimmering in the distance, the cathedral of Ely, showed him quite plainly what must be done. There must be a channel round the *outside* of the whole fen area, so that the water never reached the low-lying areas to flood them. And to solve the problem of tidal drop in the Bedford River, there must be another river, running parallel to it, which would be tidal through the sluices he needed to build. This was more than day-dreaming. It was madness. But with the certainty of years of experience in Holland, he knew that he was right.

Perhaps if he called his new river a drain, that would make it sound smaller and less expensive. And if he suggested that the Bedford River be called Old Bedford, and his new waterway the New Bedford in honour of the Earl's advancement to Duke, human vanity would succeed where practical engineering could not dent the surface.

The water was seeping through his fine leather boots, and he was aware of the wind cutting its way into his jerkin. Yes, he would hold to this vision like those strange ugly English dogs called bulldogs, which he had seen fighting, holding on to the death. If he could persuade those who had employed him, he would have solved the problem of the fens once and for all, and his name would always be remembered.

"That, Cornelius, is a strange kind of immortality you bestow on yourself. Come, you must write all this down before the idea fades away." He stumped off across the boggy peat cuttings to where he had tethered his horse. There was much to be done.

Denver Sluice: right hand gate admitting tidal water

SOME BACKGROUND SKETCHES

My father, Cyril Clarke, was Superintendent of the Waterbeach Level District from 1943 to 1974, responsible for the irrigation and drainage of more than six thousand acres of prime growing land. He will have his say in his own words later. It must be understood that I write about him as a father. I have no doubt that he was a good Superintendent, a man who knew and understood both land and water. Others may indeed write about him in that respect and will probably present a totally different picture. As I best remember him, in his middle years, he was tall, well-proportioned, with dark hair that waved in an almost Italian style and with eyes of blue-grey. From his Sennitt ancestors he inherited a heavy square jaw and a mouth that tended to turn down at the corners. Often I have heard him swear under his breath as yet another person called out to him "Cheer up, Clarkie, it can't be as bad as all that." He was born in 1909, and his death in 2008 has freed me to speak candidly of his background, something he forbade. To do that I must go back one generation further, to my paternal grandparents Linda Sennitt and Horace Clarke. When my grandmother died, my father as her only child had the job of sorting out her papers, and was astonished and more than a little distressed to discover that the date of his birth was only a month after the date of her marriage. She must almost have had him on the church steps, he said. Young Horace certainly held out against marriage to the last minute. From odd comments made during her declining years when she lived

Linda age 25

3

with us, and from photos of her as a young woman, I have put together what she did, and tried to imagine why she did it.

Florence Emily Melinda Sennitt was a beauty. Tall, slender, dark haired and possessed of a pair of eyes that could command any of the farmers' lads and other hobble-de-hoys around her to kneel at her feet, she quite clearly thought herself above them all. Her attitude was commendable while she was still in her teens, but once she crossed the threshold of her twenties and was still not only un-married but not even spoken for, matters began to look gloomy. So she went up to the Wisbech area, to the fruit gardens, to work picking plums and apples. I used to wonder why, if ever it was mentioned in the local paper, she would grunt that "All the scum of the earth come from Wisbech" and caution me never to go up there. But I am convinced that she went so far from her own village because she was planning, quite coolly and calmly, to get herself a husband, and if that meant being compromised, then I think she was quite prepared to go along that route. It was up there that she encountered a young Suffolk farm worker, Horace Clarke, who himself had a secret to hide. He was a handsome enough young man, from Brockford near Mendelsham but as his birth was some two years after his official father had died, all his life he had known the pointing finger and the taunt of illegitimacy. Perhaps after the day's fruit picking was done, the two of them exchanged confidences. In that one respect my grandparents were alike, that they scorned convention, although as a farm lad Horace must have known the facts of life. Whether Linda totally understood is another matter. But she achieved her aim.

Pregnant, and subsequently married, Linda went to live with Horace in Mendelsham where my father was born. From the start, she idolised her son. In the family photo album is a sequence of photos of him from about the age of five, posed in his best clothes which she must have scraped and saved to purchase. When the Great War broke out Horace, probably as much to get away from his wife as in the cause of patriotism, joined other keen young men at the recruiting station. My father has few memories of him, but once told me that Horace began his promotion as an NCO in the Suffolk Regiment because on the command of "Both feet RAISE" he leaped forward and hung onto the shoulders of the lad in the row in front of him. Before long he became a Company Sergeant Major and the family moved to Dovercourt near Harwich. By then, it was clear to them both that marriage had been a drastic error even if the only possible course of action. They actively hated each other.

Now comes something which I can only surmise, as there is no proof. Horace vanished during the war, Missing believed Killed. That is what I was always told. But grandmother, nodding in her chair by the fire at Engine House, would sometimes look out through the window along the road to where the bridge crossed the Old West river and say "Ah, one of these days I shall see Horace come walking along that road," and I think now that she knew he was not dead. It was easier in that war to vanish, to exchange identity discs, and plead loss of memory. Many years later I encountered someone in Mendelsham who could only have been a close relative of my father and who was puzzled by my talk of Horace being dead. "Why, no, that he weren't," he said with a frown. "He come back here after the war, Uncle Horace did, and lived with some woman or other up in London." Could it have been that Horace realised Linda would be better off with her war-widow status and her Service pension than to continue married to him? Linda's elder brother Sidney lived in London, and it seems that after the War, Linda would sometimes go to stay with them. Was she, perhaps, visiting the man who was, after all, still her lawfully wedded husband? It ties in with her strange character. We shall never know the truth, because all those involved are long dead and the records, such as they are, only relate the official story

Whatever the reason, Linda, who had a vicious temper and could, so her father apparently said, pick a quarrel with the side of the wash-house if there was no-one else around, soon disagreed with her Suffolk in-laws, brought her young son back to Stretham, to her parents, where she dumped him and went off to find work that would support them both. I know that she spent some time working in Addenbrookes Hospital as an auxiliary, because many years later she would still speak with great respect of Sister Tebbutt who must have been her superior. She also spent time as a cleaner at The Leys School. But to all intents and purposes my father was brought up by his grandparents.

It is time for his voice to be heard. What follows is taken from tapes he recorded during the early 1970's.

Old Stretham

"Perhaps you wonder what the village of Stretham was like years ago. Much of it was thatched and colour washed, quite picturesque, of course. The characters who lived there were real village types. There were the huge family of Murfitts. All, I suppose, in some way related, and yet as far apart as, shall we say, oh, chalk from cheese or something like that. And they were known by their various family names. There were, for instance, the Bucket Murfitts, the Buddle Murfitts, they were all one family and they all had fair curly hair, don't ask me why, I don't know why. There were the Huckle Murfitts who were a little bit above the others, they owned their own house, and their own business, they were coal merchants. Then there were the Tickeypotts, don't know how they got that name, but I knew the old lady, a very nice old lady too, anyway …. Now so far we've had the Buddles, the Buckets, the Huckles and the Tickeypotts .. oh, and of course there were the Clark Murfitts – yes, they were farmers. My granny used to go plucking for them. These Clark Murfitts used to sell poultry, eggs and such-like, to the University or, as they said, to the Colleges. My granny used to go plucking, used to sit in an old shed, covered in old clothes and bags [hessian sacks] and pluck and prepare the chickens and geese every week for this man to take to the Colleges. .And that brings me to think of the carrier's cart.

There were two carriers' carts in Stretham when I was a boy. When my mother was in hospital at one time for 15 weeks it meant that Granny and I used to go to Cambridge quite a bit by carriers cart. So this was an ordinary cart, two wheels, with a hood, a canvas hood, built on a frame and fixed on the sides, and there we would sit, and coming home of course at night we used to leave Cambridge at 4 in the wintertime and it would be pitch dark long before we got home. You see not only did this person, Mrs Sennitt her name was, take passengers to Cambridge – and she would have a load, there would be her driving the horse, there would be, I suppose, three people down one side and three up the back and three the other side, that's nine people, ten with her. We'd leave Stretham at I suppose approximately half past seven on a Saturday morning, and we would probably get to Cambridge, what, oh I don't know, say half past ten. You see, it wasn't only passengers that this Mrs Sennitt took in her cart, there was eggs and butter and cream and probably some poultry too, all for the colleges, and on the way you see she seldom went more than half a mile without stopping at some farm to pick up more produce. And then when she got to there we, the passengers would relax, and do our various jobs we'd come for. But Mrs Sennitt, she'd be rushing around to various chemists, grocers, dressmakers shops for things which she'd had ordered by people living in Stretham. "Would you get me such and such when you go to Cambridge … get me a yard of this cloth … get me something from the chemists." Coming home we would do the same as we did when we went. We would stop at every farmhouse we came to along the road and she would nip out and up the garden path and knock on the door, and a light would appear, and she would hand over this parcel, collect a few pence for it and on we would jog with just the dim light of two, I suppose candle lamps they would be, big candles of course in special holders on the side of the vehicle. As a boy I remember watching the shadows of the spokes of the wheels in the candle light. And of course there was no other traffic on the road. Sometimes a spanking gig would pass us with a beautiful cob, you know, at breakneck speed, and we would look on in admiration and perhaps envy as this man going to Cambridge market flew past us and doing, probably, 6 or 8 mph, and this of course was the only people on the road in those days. I remember when the first motor car came through Stretham, strangely enough I think it was a Rolls and it belonged to a big lady landowner and farmer who lived at Witchford and us boys rushed to the wall in the school yard and gazed at this motor car. There was a very elegant chauffeur driving, dressed in navy blue with a peaked cap and we made a lot of that, you can bet.

Anyway, I seem to have strayed a bit. I did promise to tell you about our village. I have said that at least half of it was thatched and the other half, the newer half, was built after the disastrous fire which occurred, so my grandfather used to tell me, in a blacksmith's shop in one of the back streets, roared through half the village and I suppose in the end burnt itself out. Or they probably had to pull down some buildings to make a fire-break.

Grandfather could tell me some rare stories. He remembered when the stagecoach used to come through and stop at the Red Lion. He was a small boy and used to be paid to lead the horses into the stables which I believe are still there. And for instance how the hangman came to Stretham. I think he was on his way to Lynn. Of course grandfather, John Sennitt, was a bit of a mess himself, he had only one hand and he was born that way. Strangely enough there were two of them in the village, two and a boy of my own age when I was a boy. They had the arm as far as the wrist and yet no hand. Oh, he was a big man, and he had phenomenal strength. He could do more things with that stump than people with both hands could do. He wore a strap and he made that act as his other hand. He could mow; he could even run a wheelbarrow. Now you may well say that's impossible with one hand, well he would put a cord over the handle of the barrow and get his stump underneath it, so he could lift it. One of the things of course he wasn't able to do was sharpen a scythe. You think about that – you see you have to hold a scythe with one hand and rub the blade with a rub-stone with the other hand. But he could do a wonderful lot of things. And eating, he had a special knife made for him, it's up with the Cutler's Company in London now, it was like a cheese knife with a kind of prong on the end of the curve, but the back of it was sharpened like a knife, so you see he would cut with the sharp edge, then pick up his food with the prong, and that was all very wonderful to me.

He would also tell me of the far-off days when he would read the newspapers to a party of people at the Red Lion. You may well say "How the Dickens did he know how to read, in those days?" Well, he was taught by the daughter of the resident Rector of Stretham, a Rev. Baber, to whom my grandfather always owed more than one tremendous debt. And he recognised it. Although he was not what I would call a religious man, he had a wonderful affection and respect for the Rev. Baber and his daughter, who taught him as a small boy to read and write, a thing which you see many children couldn't afford, and he, I suppose, being a bit of an outcast, a bit of an oddity in the village, he would never have been able to afford it. But you see there was no place for helplessness, for thinking of things you couldn't do. You jolly well had to do it, you had to muck in with other people.

I'm going to stop here to show you something. This bell. I was always forbidden to touch it. Once, grandfather lifted it carefully from the slice of apple wood where it was balanced – you see it wouldn't sit straight because of the clapper - and put it down beside me. "There," he said. "Now you just try picking that up." I couldn't move it, even with two hands. As you can see, the handle is of some polished turned wood, it has a brass collar and the bell itself is about – oh, I should reckon about eight inches across. The clapper's made of iron, with a ball at the end to strike the rim of the bell and make the ring tone, and it's bolted into a heavy staple in the roof of the bell cavity. The body of it is made of bell metal, a carefully blended alloy of copper and tin. Grandfather told me about it – a specialist skill. Once the molten metal reached white-hot, the furnaceman would dip out a sample and pour it into a shallow depression formed in casting sand. When cool it was broken in half. If the grain of the metal was fine, the bell could be cast. Too coarse, then more tin had to be added. He knew a lot, did my Grandfather.

The only identifying mark on the bell is the number 13 and the letters WH carved into its shoulder. If it was part of a set of hand bells, it must have been the tenor bell. But this bell was not used for practising change-ringing. It needed a strong man to make it ring.

Grandfather told me how one day he was at the Rectory having his lesson from Miss Baber, the rector's daughter. A Rectory Garden Party had to be postponed. He was given the Rectory tea-bell and told to go round the village announcing the cancellation. "Postponed" was too much for him, and he ended up by shouting in a sturdy 14-year-old's voice that the Garden Party was "put off until another time". Such was the success of this that, as soon as he grew strong enough to heft it, he was given a proper bell and taught the traditional cry of "Oyez, oyez, oyez – this is to give notice that …" He cried many things; the visit of a famous Wesleyan preacher to the village, the Share-Out of the Helping Hand Club at one of the village pubs, the distribution of monies and goods from the two village Charity Foundations, the times of meetings at the Mission Hall, Sunday School treats, Whist drives. Sometimes more sadly, it would be a house clearance after a death.

On Christmas morning he would delight in opening the casement window of the bedroom and roaring out in a passable baritone a couple of verses of "Christians Awake" while Grannie Susan would be tugging at his nightshirt and saying "Come yew in, John, do." To which he would reply that Christmas should be cried first thing in the morning. Sitting in his ladder-back chair at the round table, the oil lamp drawn close so that he could read the new message, he would often tease whoever had brought it, pretending to mis-read the facts. But he was always gentle. Because of the kindness shown him his loyalty was to the Church, but he took care not to offend Chapel sensitivities, and a piece of home-made toffee was handed out before the messenger left. He didn't charge very much – one shilling was the price for some twenty announcements in various parts of the village, a price that never varied however long the notice.

I've just mentioned my Granny – a small [when I say small I mean short, round, she was round] person who, when I think about her now, well, she was like a large russet apple. She was a wonderful little person. God rest her soul. She taught me how to tell the time with Roman numerals that of course were on every clock in the Kingdom in those days, a little bit difficult for a small boy 5 or 6 years old. Confusing. But anyway she taught me that, and she taught me my ABC. You may well say what did I learn at school – well, precious little. School was a funny place and I didn't like it much. I suppose for that same reason they didn't like me, and so they didn't force things on me. I was a bit of a dreamer, and I went to so many schools, my education was split up. I went to Mendelsham school in Suffolk and Stretham, depending on whether my mother had had another row with the family. Sometimes they'd put me on the train with a label on my coat and the Guard, he'd look after me and see I got to Stretham all right, and then I had a mile and a half to walk to the village. But there you are, that was life. Oh, and at one point I went to school in a garrison town near Harwich called Dovercourt while my father was there, and for a little while too I was even at the prep department of Oundle school. Because I remember being in that great big church and being auditioned, and singing in the choir. I don't know why we were living in Oundle, but we were.

I'm still talking to you about the old village, am I not. And my Granny. On a Friday night I used to look forward to going off to get the meat. Of course it was on a Friday night because that was the night my grandfather got paid. It seems extraordinary, his pay of what – 16 bob, maybe. And so there we would go, granny and I, and if it was terribly dark I'd be allowed to carry the lantern, and we'd go up Pump Lane. It was called that because at the end was the village pump and there would always be people round that, day or night, winter or summer, spring or autumn, you could always be certain there'd be someone at the village pump. In fact the people who lived round this pump registered many a complaint about people making a lot of noise after nightfall around the pump. I suppose these poor beggars needed water, didn't they, whatever the time of day or night.

Anyway, we would go to the butchers, Charlie Parnell's, and I'd gaze quite fascinated while this man cut off the meat. They used to sell dripping in those days, people used a lot of dripping, they used to render it down from the carcasses. And when the fat was rendered down, there'd be little crunchy bit of fat left over rather like porky scratchings you can still get today. So I'd seen some of my mates eating these things, and I begged my granny to let me have some, and I've never been so disappointed in my life. Usually she'd buy me a pennyworth of sweets, and I suppose I thought there would take the place of these sweets, and you can imagine my disappointment, these things tasted like a lot of old flannel, I chewed them and chewed them and I never asked for them again.

There was always one little aspect that rather saddened me about these visits. On our way to the butchers we would pass – well, for want of a better word, a one-up, one-down shack. and it was used, when I was a boy, as a saddlers, a harness makers shop. My granny would sometimes look at it, and she would say, 'that was poor old mother's house. That was where poor old mother died` or something like that. And she would wipe away a genuine tear. She was a very soft-hearted person. She could laugh and cry at the same time. And by and by I wormed out of her the story of this mother of hers. Apparently there were two girls and a crippled boy, and the crippled boy made his living by being a shepherd. He looked after sheep. Well, of course he did, and I don't know why I bothered to tell you that. He could do that because they supplied him with a donkey to ride on. And then there were these two girls. And their father died rather young. These girls were in their teens and of course there was no widow's pension, there was no nothing, they had to get food and live as best they could. The parish, I believe, supplied them with so many pounds of flour per person per week but to supplement this, the mother used to go to work, to work like a man, cutting corn with a sickle, doing all kinds of work on a farm which she could possibly do. And she wore herself out, there's no other explanation to it. She died – I suppose she would be between 30 and 40, worn out. And I remember my granny telling me that she and her sister sat and watched their mother die and they had nothing in the house to give her. And I thought this was very sad but I suppose it was only one of many. We talk of the good old days, but they weren't so very good, were they? They were pretty tough. Those had it had the lot and those that had nothing had even less than nothing.

Anyway, let's not get carried away with such thoughts.

There was another carrier's cart. A Mrs Dimmock who ran a carriers cart. I never travelled in her cart, I don't know why but it probably had something to do with the name of Sennitt, because the cart we used to ride in was run by Mrs. Sennitt. My grandfather was a Sennitt, and we do go back in the village a long, long way. It is supposed that we come from a family of puritans who settled in the village many years ago and it is a distortion of Sen-night – Sabbath night. This, I suppose, is very possible. Anyway, there was quite a family of these Sennitts in the village when I was a boy. They didn't pretend to be relations, but I suppose they must have been right at the back of the rootstock. My grandfather's family was quite a large one – they were, in those days – and his father was killed by being struck by lightning. This used to happen, I won't say a lot, but it did used to happen in the countryside. Anyhow, that was how he was killed. This meant, of course, that the family split up. I never heard him refer much to his family, and he, I think, left home as soon as ever he was able, and he went to live as a very young man, little more than a boy, with a somewhat distant relation of his and he was always full of praise for this relation, Sam Green, and I think he was a Sennitt Green or his wife had probably been a Sennitt. Anyway, I do remember one thing, I can remember this old man and old woman, Mr and Mrs Green, little people they were, but then there used to be lots of little people in our village that that time, but I'll tell you something else, I can remember at least three old men who were literally bent double, I suppose with arthritis, or rheumatism or something, caused through getting wet at work and keeping wet clothes on, I don't know why it was but you never see this today, do you. But you could see it when I was a boy, men who certainly never saw the stars because they couldn't. They couldn't stand upright. They walked with two sticks, and looked very pathetic, but of course they were just figures of fun for us old boys, I'm afraid.

Any rate … when old Sam Green died, there was a sale of his furniture, and I suppose partly out of sentiment, and probably because he badly needed a table, my grandfather made up his mind that he was going to buy this table, and I remember it well as I suppose most of my family do. It was an ordinary white-wood table and my mother had put some kind of hideous black stain on the legs My mother used to tell me that he carried this table home on his head, and this was always a laugh, Sam Green's table. But when you come to think of it, I suppose he kind of got inside the four legs, because of his only having one hand, and supported the underneath of the table on his head and held one of the legs with his good hand, because as I've said he was a big man, and strong, and once loaded up like that he could have easily walked from Grunty Fen where the Greens lived to Middle Street in Stretham. But there you are.

Getting back to the Great Fire, I've just remember that hanging on the wall of one of the buildings pretty well in the centre of the High Street were two long-handled iron hooks, which puzzled me for a long time, what they were and what they were for and so on, and then I was told that they were for pulling burning thatch off buildings. It was one of the only ways they had in those days of combating fire. Otherwise they would have to go to the village pump for buckets of water.

Well, still on this subject of carriers cart, there was another type of carrier in the village known as Ted Lowe who had lost his hand in an accident with a chaff-cutter and he carried out an existence – it must have been a pretty grim one too – he had an old horse and a two-wheeled cart and he would run errands for people between Ely and Stretham. If you wanted anything fetching from Ely, you went and saw Mr. Lowe and you paid him a few pence and gave him your order for the next day. I remember his poor old horse died and of course he hadn't enough money to buy another one and so they collected round the village for him. In fact I remember two people coming to the door and saying 'So and So's horse has died, and we're having a collection' and they'd collect a few pence here and there and perhaps a shilling, which so they would be able to buy this man another horse. So there was a sort of a more friendly atmosphere in the village in those days.

There were two days which the girls used to look forward to very much. One was May Day, the other was St. Valentine's day. Now on May Day they would dress a doll in all its finest raiment and they would make a cradle probably of rushes or their father might perhaps make them a willow basketwork affair, and they would deck this with all kinds of wild flowers – the countryside was at its best then – and I may tell you here that I can remember when we had a lot of wonderful flowers in the village. There were violets galore in the hedge bottoms, there was crowsfoot, as we called it, which was a little orchid, paigles, which was our name for cowslips and buttercups, daisies, wild honeysuckle in the hedges of Berry Green I can remember vivid ly, because the scent used to creep right down into the village on a June night. They'd exhibit this doll and this cradle and the Rector's wife would admire it, and maybe pick it up and look at it very intently and give them another copper or a bun or an apple, whatsoever she had.

The other one was St. Valentines Day, and they'd be dressed up proper fine, and with some flowers in their hair, I suppose it would be coltsfoot or celandines and perhaps some very early wild plum blossom, and they'd knock on the door and say the following poem to the woman who came to the door:

Good morning, good morning, Valentine
Dress your hair as I do mine.

Then the householder would give them a half-penny, or a penny, each and off they'd go delighted.

For us boys and for many generations of boys in Stretham there used to be something called Plough Monday, early in January. And us boys used to rush about like mad on that day, we'd go to all the big farmers, and little ones too, and we would be paid a penny or halfpenny and with these we would buy sugar, and then my granny used to make black balls. She'd put this brown sugar in a saucepan and boil it up and make a kind of toffee, sticky and sweet and lovely for a small boy.

I've just remembered two very strange things regarding the collections around the village. I know they intrigued me as a small boy. One was for the weathercock on top of the church steeple, which blew down or had perhaps been taken down by the village postman who was a great climber. Anyway they collected round the village to have this weathercock repaired and put back again. I was intrigued by the size of this bird. And I remember they came round collecting for was for a set of false teeth for a poor widow with a large family, strange to collect for this.

But of course, the great thing that was the central life of the village was the village Feast. This was held on the third Sunday in May, and it was quite an event. There was a big service in church and there used to be a parade headed by a band from one of the nearby villages. My grandfather used to call it The Annual Muck-out, because lots of people who had never worn their Sunday clothes since the last Feast would put them on and turn out to watch this procession. Our village never had a band, I don't think we were very musical. Then would come the big Friendly Society banner, the Order of Ancient Shepherds, and they would be in all their glory, they had all sorts of decorations and medals, and big gauntlets and carried silver crooks, and this big banner with a huge red cross on it. Following them would come or perhaps three horse-drawn wagons. The horses would be beautifully dressed up – their manes would be braided and they would have all sorts of brasses collected from every farmer in the village, topknots and brass topknots and haimes for the collars and brushes on their backs, their tails done up in ribbons and the whole thing was very wonderful to us lads at this time. And of course the man in charge of each horse would be a very proud person. Inside the wagons there would be people dressed up, portraying probably a scene from the bible, oh, the Good Samaritan or something like that, or a scene from a hospital ward, a bed with a patient all powdered up, one or two buxom lasses as nurses and a man would be dressed in frock coat and top hat as a doctor. There would be collections, of course, all the way along the village streets, and this money, together with the money that was collected at the band concert held in the evening in the main street, this would to Addenbrookes hospital in Cambridge, and then you see after all this affair, about nine o'clock on the Sunday evening the big showmens' engines would roll into the village, terribly impressive. And they would take their stand where they were going to have their roundabouts.

They used to stop up the Ely Road – of course, this was long before the by-pass was built – and fill up their water tanks from Pitch Pond. I suppose that was quite a deep pond, because us kids were always told never to play near it, as it had no bottom. Well, that's impossible, but we believed it and it was always a mysterious sort of place, surrounded by tall trees. I wonder now if it could have been a pit dug to provide the footings for the windmill what stood just opposite, because it had very steep sides and to me that means something dug, not just something that happened like a dew pond in a field corner. And you could always tell where a dew pond had been even if in later years that field was under the plough, because they just couldn't get rid of the dip, and the crop, whatever they were growing, would always be affected in that corner.. Wheat and barley would tend to rot, and sugar beet would grow juicier. But I don't know why I'm telling you things like that, which won't be of any interest.

Early on Monday morning there would be a real old knocking and banging and they would have the whole lot erected so that they could open the Feast by 12 midday And there they would be, the galloping horses, stalls selling gingerbread, stalls selling rock and my mother could remember when they used to sell prunes. Something I can't remember. And she and my granny used to talk about frumitty, which I think was a kind of porridge made of cracked wheat grains boiled until they were soft and sticky. It would be like we have candyfloss these days, something sweet and filling for the kids and not costing much. I can remember cheapjacks selling watches at a shilling each; well of course they never went. Silver spoons, shilling a bundle, you got them home and put them in some boiling water they were just lead, black as your hat, still – that didn't matter, they set out to catch you and you were well and truly caught.

Then the Rock King would be shouting away, wearing a big Stetson hat and a white suit, with a large, very large, watch chain, looked to us kids like solid gold and probably was, I don't know. And he would sell rock, 'Half a pound of nougat and half a pound of rock, shilling, who wants a bag full, 'ere you are my dear` and then he would throw a handful of sweets across the grass. Then there'd be a hustle and a bustle and us old boys would scrap about picking them up, dust, that wouldn't make any difference, we'd whip them into us, and so life was very pleasant at Stretham Feast.

I do remember one thing which does seem to be very strange in these hygienic days. Even in those days I didn't think a lot of it. They were called squibs, they were metal containers about the size or a little bigger than a large size toothpaste tube. Two feast women, sleeves rolled up, leather aprons, would fill these things with mucky water which us old boys had got previously from the pond, I know this because I've helped to get it, in a barrel on two wheels. Well, fair enough, no harm in that was there, we got it from the village pond. And you squirted this at people and no-one really became all that unfriendly about it. I remember one girl who used to have to go home perhaps twice a night to change her underclothes. I suppose you could say she was popular.

I remember too my grandfather telling me of his days as a lad, going to Ely Fair. Now that was a rough old how do ye do in them days, gangs fighting each other, they didn't need to get drunk to have a good old scrap, they'd plan it all year. And he was specially at risk because of his having only one hand. Well, of course they walked into Ely from all the surrounding villages in those days. And he and some of the Stretham lads knew that a gang from, I think it was Witchford or somewhere were waiting just where the Isle of Ely drops back into the fen again, they call it Brickle Hill, or they did then. From the Brick Kilns. And grandfather hadn't even a stick to defend himself with, and of course they didn't carry knives. Not village boys. But he'd bought himself a poke of steamed winkles in their shells off one of the stalls, to eat when he got home, so he took off his red neckercher, put this poke of winkles in it and tied it up in a knot. You may ask how someone with only one hand could tie a knot, well he could use his good hand and his teeth to tie a knot in anything except his neck-tie, and that Granny had to fix for him. Which was why he wore a neckercher, because he could just wrap that round inside his shirt collar. But anyway, he made this improvised weapon, and he used that as a sort of swinging club to whirl round his head and keep this other lot at bay until his mates could make a run for it. I told you, he was a big man. And he told me he broke one chap's nose, and that chap went round with a crooked nose for the rest of his life.

Which makes me remember another little set-up he told me about. I'd been out in the fen with my mates round one of what we called the fossil pits, and brought a couple of the coprolites home. Nowadays they tell us these are fossilised dinosaur dung but to me they were just curiosities, funny shaped black stones. I showed them to Grandfather, and he told me a bit about the fossil-digging which happened in the mid 19th century, and how the stones were ground up to make fertiliser. How he'd done a bit of fossil-digging as a lad, for pocket money, and together with a few rough characters that the digging industry had attracted, the grown men decided to have a fair of their own at Upware. 'They called it The Upware Bustle' he said. There was a lot to drink, one man had made himself King of the Fair and offered a reward to any man who could drink down the whole contents of a huge earthenware pot, then be put into a boat on the river without any oars and paddle his way back with his hands in so many minutes.' He stretched out his maimed arm and looked at it, and said 'That weren't for me, of course.' I listened with a delicious little thrill as he told about the amount they all drank, the dancing and – as he put it – courting that went on and the fights that broke out all over the river bank. Then I asked him if anyone had called the Police. He gave me a considering, old-fashioned look and thought for a minutes. 'I don't know as I should be telling you this,' he said slowly. 'And I don't want you to think you can be doing things like that today. That was nigh fifty years ago, and I was just a lad.' I begged him to go on. 'Well,' grudgingly, 'two policemen did come along. The one from Wicken was pitched head-first into the Lode, and the Upware man went backwards into the main drain. After that we didn't hear too much from them, and in the end we all got tired of rushing about, and the drink ran out, so we went home.'

So anyway, in our day we had these squibs, and there was another stall that sold confetti by the bag full, so you were slopped all over with this dirty water and then had a handful of confetti thrown over you. So the whole thing had a bizarre tone, very much like a fair in America, the whole High Street was alive with people laughing at the most obstreperous things, and no one caring a damn. Happy! And there was 'tiddle-em-ups' which were made of long streamers of paper fixed into some kind of handle. And most people wore funny hats, or a funny nose, or something like that. It was a gala affair.

Then came WW1 and the Feast stopped, because you see there was no sugar for the rock and there was no coal for the engines. And so we had a break of two or three years, and after the War it started up again but there was a difference, looking back, a vast difference. We still had the Feast, still the roundabouts, still the stalls, coconut shy, the swing boats, the rock, but it was more civilized. That's a strange word. And of course I was growing up and the men who'd come back from France had seen new things …."

Across the years I remember my father stopping the tape there, and gazing out of the window. I sensed his mood and tiptoed out, leaving an old man with his memories.

THE VILLAGE OF STRETHAM

The village that my father knew as a boy was very different from what you might see today if you visited. In those days it was laid out almost on an American grid pattern, with Front Street, Middle Street and Back Lane, crossed at the top by Top Street. Pump Lane ran from the village pump into Middle Street, and Chapel Lane across into Back Lane. Pond Street completed the square at the bottom, so called because it passed by the official village pond, and going the other way it was called Wilburton Road. The corner where these roads met was called Hall Corner, on account of the Mission Hall which was built in 1884, and where according to father, grandfather and the local lads would sing very scurrilous words to some of the Sankey and Moody hymns then so popular.

Hold the fort, for I am coming, Satan's cut his throat
See the blood run down his whiskers, onto his Sunday coat

Or even

Hold the fort, for I am coming, in a donkey cart
The wheels are loose, the shafts are bent.
The donkey's going to ….

Also, it seems, the 1880's being the time when bustles gave way to bell skirts, it was the done thing to 'jostle' the young ladies attending the services as they came in, to see if you could make their skirts turn up and reveal their petticoats. Nothing much seems to change!

Stretham, the 'ham' on the 'stret', in other words the Saxon settlement built on the old Roman Road Akeman Street, was purchased by Ethelwold, Bishop of Winchester, and presented to the monks of Ely. Other people have written books about the village, including Stretham, a Feast of Memories by my aunt Beatrice Stevens and a comprehensive guide prepared by Stretham Parish Council at the Millennium. We lived out of the village down a road called Green End. I remember the road well from the many journeys I made along it, in sun and rain, in bitter frosty weather with my thighs smarting in the wind, late at night after some assignation in one of the fields that bordered it, very early in the morning during the year I worked in Cambridge. I could probably tell you, even now so many years later, the position of each pothole and puddle.

Let's take the road from the village end, as it was then at least. The first part of the left hand side was easy enough - it was the allotment gardens which, in that productive soil, yielded heavy crops and were also used for growing flowers for the market. Strawberries too - when it was berry time us kids would always get off our bikes at the allotment gate and hang around, waiting to be told we could come and pick off the last little berries on a row which had been all but stripped. Some of the allotment holders would deliberately leave one or two big ones for us to find. But the right hand side of the road was a bit more interesting. The last house on that side was Charlie Clark's, and he had an orchard in which was a flock of weird, wonderful guineafowl with their penetrating cry of 'Come-back, Come-back'. After that was a short straight bit that went past King Cob, a field with a mysterious ruined house in it where there were gooseberry bushes and currants during the summer, but also the threat of a ghost - no doubt to keep us kids off the fruit. Then came Reg Sennitt's field, where he kept his cows which would often be meandering along the road up to his milking parlour, stopping all the traffic while they munched their way home. His field had some of the longest stemmed daisies around, and his daughter Ann, a very distant cousin of mine on my father's side, would sit with me piercing and threading the flowers during the Spring half term holiday to put round the necks of our dolls. Round the corner now, and on the left was Goodge's sheds, a ramshackle collection of former Nissen huts and animal pens. Then Everitt's Drove which had a field along it where crested newts were to be found in Spring, and where I experienced my first kiss - but that was much later. After the drove entry, the way was marked with trees - a big ash tree, then half a field further on an even bigger wych-elm, and finally across the Cut with the elm scrub around it where goat moths used to lay their eggs. Then, at last, blessed shelter with Gotobed's hedge one side and Jack Day's orchard shielding from the east wind. Up the slope of the bridge and over the river, and home was in sight. But there were two potholes in the road which, however often filled, always opened up again and they had to be avoided before I could swoop down the slope in front of our house and sling my bike against the window in the passage beside the house.

I always wondered why that window was there, and why it had frosted glass in half of it, as there was another large window on the other side of the kitchen - as we called the room we lived in. It had been put there, I was told, so that the Superintendent could pay his men direct without them coming into the house, and the frosted glass was so that no-one could see into the room. To pay the men, he would simply push up the bottom half of the window and hand the money out. Incredibly feudal it now seems, but when the house was built such things were taken for granted.

Engine House, built in 1901, was far and away too grand for the likes of us. But it went with the job, and as I was only 18 months old when we moved there, I thought of it as home. It had been considered too grand for at least one of the previous Superintendents, Mr. Houseley, who ran the district from 1884 to 1930. He lived in the wash-house once the new house was built, and on one occasion when ill-health forced him to be in bed in the new house, one of the Commissioners who were his employers was compelled to climb up a ladder and talk to him through the window, as Houseley's militant housekeeper would tolerate no dirty boots!

The house was big, L-shaped, and had deep sash windows. The L-shaped part contained the kitchen, scullery and pantry, with a coal-bunker and a galvanised steel porch tucked on the back. The front of the house, which faced the road, had the lounge to the west side and father's study to the east, with a front door which, in best Fen traditions, was never opened. Visitors came down the passage and round to the back door.

Many years later, when I was at Ely High School, a homosexual scandal occurred in the local Secondary Modern school. I think it was of a very mild nature, but it caused parents to fold their mouths up and refuse to discuss it. So we Sixth-formers consulted the biggest Oxford diction-ary we could find in the local library and came up with the definition of a homosexual as one who "has relations via the back passage". As all our relations tended to visit 'round the back' we couldn't, for the life of us, see why this had caused such an outcry.

Down the yard was a row of outhouses, the top one simply called 'the shed', the middle one the wash-house where the copper was, and also a large grain-bin for the chickens which we kept for many years. The tin bath hung on the wall, and occurs again shortly afterwards, my mother had a paraffin-fired stove with an oven that sat across two of the burners, so that she could cook in summer without making the house too hot. Until I was about twelve years old, we lived in what would today be considered primitive circumstances. We had no running water, no electricity. The cooking was done in the kitchen on an old, black-leaded Herald Range. Summer was pleas-ant enough, but winter was gripping; I was allowed to come downstairs to get dressed in front of the fire. On Saturday and Sunday evenings we would go either into the Lounge or the Study for the evening. A fire would be lit there and I shudder to think what Health and Safety would have made of the way that was done. Mother would simply get the grate ready with kindling sticks and paper, then carry a shovel-full of red hot coals from the kitchen into whichever room we were intending to use and shoot them on to the sticks. Had she tripped, the whole house could easily have caught fire! In the winter, in spite of hot water bottles and feather beds to snuggle into, the bedroom pot used to freeze over and there would be enough frost on the window panes to scratch patterns in, though that wasn't an occupation I used to spend much time at.

The problem with getting water to us was the old wooden bridge across the Old West at the end of Green End Road. It just wouldn't have stood the weight of a water-main. So finally it was demolished and a new concrete structure put in its place, and the great day came when we had water from the tap and a flushing toilet. Though in our case they had to adapt what had been the coal-store to house the downstairs loo. No doubt you will be wondering what we had done before then. We had a family three-holer down the yard, two large holes and one small one for me; the loo paper was the Radio Times or sometimes The Farmers Weekly, each page torn in half and threaded on a string to be hung on a nail. Remember, we are talking about the 1950's here, not Victorian times. Just outside, fed from the slate roof of the privy, was a large water but and one simply dipped one's hands in there and shook the water off by way of hygiene. And about every four years my poor father had the job of emptying the cess-pit under the wooden seat, and burying the contents in a trench in the cornfield just the other side of the garden fence, a job from which I was kept well away. I think the clothes he wore for the job were burned afterwards, right down to the skin, which is not surprising.

Until the running water came, we bathed once a week. I had the first go, and Mother topped up my bath water and used it herself while a second copper-full of water was made ready for father. All this was done in the washhouse.

When the water was laid on, a new, rather splendid fireplace with a low basket type fire and two ovens, in pale green stove enamel, was installed where the old range had been. Mother was delighted with it, because it needed no black-lead polishing and to a great degree was reliable for baking. The Commissioners came round to view the new installations. Mother and I, believe it or not, were half hiding behind the scullery door as the party came past, and the Chairman poked at her with his walking stick and said in his nasal, aristocratic drawl "Y'arl be wantin' electricity next, I suppose," to which she was too much in awe of him to reply.

How did we light the place? Upstairs, it was candles. We each had our own candlestick to take up to bed. And of course we washed downstairs, so there wasn't what my father would have called 'a lot of blundering about in the dark'. In the kitchen and the two front rooms we had lamps with incandescent mantles, a gentle light, one standing on the table in summer and one hanging from the ceiling in winter. What a to-do if the asbestos mantle grew too hot and started to 'black' – the lamp had to be turned down until the correct temperature had been achieved once again.

Engine House kitchen, showing mother, new stove and lamp

It was not until after I had left home to be a student in London that power was finally coaxed across the fens, and that was because the big farmers had clamoured for power for their grain dryers. Once the cable was up, it was a simple matter of putting in a step-down transformer and life became relatively normal. But that is not for this story.

You may be wondering what the job of a fen drainage Superintendent entailed. Before we go into that, we need a definition of the Fens, and in particular the black fens where the soil is peat. For this I am indebted to the definitive work by A K Astbury entitled The Black Fens, and from which I now quote.

'The black peat fens of the Isle of Ely are an interesting area for a number of reasons. The fact that their soil is vegetable and not mineral has had decisive effects on the lives and work of all who live in the area. In the building of houses, the laying of roads, the draining of land and the cultivation of the soil, the peats of the southern fens have dictated a pattern of living entirely different from that obtaining elsewhere in England; and in that respect alone, the black fens are unique. They are unique also in that they are disappearing. Their surface soil, sinking at anything up to two inches a year as a result of the wasting of the peat fibres, will within perhaps another century have ceased to exist. The fens are therefore not only a phenomenon – they are a phenomenon doomed to extinction.'

The silt fens, 730 square miles, form a well-developed area east of a line drawn between Wisbech and Boston by way of Spalding and Donington. South and west of them are the 570 square miles of the peat fens, broken only by gravel or clay islands such as Ely or March and lesser gravel mounds on one of which the village of Stretham was built. The difference between the two types of fen is that when peat is drained, it shrinks. Some say it shrinks by the height of a man during the life of a man. Wastage and sinking of the peat means that over wide areas the land is below sea level, meaning that the rivers run well above land level. At times of high water this can create a dangerous situation. Fen rivers are different from those in most of the rest of England in that they are embanked, enclosing wide areas of what is known as washland to form an emergency catchment for high water until it can be released into the sea again. In the case of the river Ouse, this is at Denver. Most rivers, when they flood, simply spill over their edges, taking the line of least resistance, and once the water feeding them has subsided they return naturally to their courses. In the fens, once the washland basin is full, there is the permanent threat of the banks "blowing", in other words being ripped open by water pressure. The flood water then pours out into the fen, spreading until it meets some kind of barrier such as a railway embankment, a metalled road which has over the years been built up above land level, or eventually the gradual slopes of the edges of the fen basin. The breached bank must be mended before any kind of pumping operation can take place, and only then can the land be reclaimed.

So the job of a Drainage Superintendent is really to maintain the ideal conditions in a vast vegetable sponge, letting water in by way of sluices in early summer so that the crops will grow and flourish, lifting water out in late winter and spring so that the land is not waterlogged. It is no wonder that one of my first memories is being told "Sshhh, it's the weather forecast!" at five minutes to six in the evening, because where, and when, heavy rain might occur would have an immediate effect on my father's next few days, since the black fens are the 'sink' of more than a dozen counties.

Later on he will be telling us some of the facts. Meanwhile, here is an expanded version of something that happened to him during the great floods of 1947. There are many tales about that great inundation, including the one where my mother, all of 4ft 10ins, tried to row a boat from the Engine House up to the village and got stuck on top of a twelve-foot high hedge. Was the reality more dramatic than the tale I have spun around it? No-one has ever spoken out about some of the dramas that were played out in the dark, small groups of men fighting to the bitter end only to see their work destroyed. Though there is no proof of disobedience, water from the breached Wissey bank did force its way through a badly blocked culvert beneath the Southery Road. And my father did write in his diary the words about being deserted by the authorities but fighting the water to the end.

BATTLE OF THE BANKS

A March evening in the wicked year of 1947, midnight plus or minus an hour. The breaking of winter's grip. Dark, icy cold. An Engineer and Foreman stand on the high bank of the fenland River Wissey. On one side of them the floodwater presses threateningly against the solid clay structure, on the other is a fifteen foot drop. If the bank gives way, millions of tons of water will pour through into the fen. All around men are at work on barricades of sandbags, with blue clay, with tarpaulins, to hold back destruction from the land that is their livelihood.

Out of the darkness a man squelches towards them. "You'd better come and look"

."What's happened now?"

"Up by Willow Farm. The back of the bank's slid into the fen."

"How far?"

"Sixty foot length."

No hope, not now. Nothing remains to stop disaster but a narrow strip, perhaps two feet wide; already the water spilling across that delicate barrier, the earth starting to crack. The weight of a single man would break it down, inevitably sweeping him to his death. But the foreman turns to the engineer.

"Just say the word, and I'll have a go."

Don't be stupid. I'm not having you killed. Get to the nearest field telephone, contact the Fen Office. If Denver Sluice stays bottled up then to be honest, mate, we might as well pack up here and go home, while we have a home to go to.

In the Fen Office in Ely another couple of men stood talking. "Breach that bank," the Chief Engineer said, pointing to a wall map, "and it'll be like a row of dominoes tumbling over. There'll be no stopping things."

"So what do we do?"

"What worries me is the main road, at right angles to the floodwater. We *must* stop the water there, or thousands of acres will be lost."

His young assistant replied thoughtfully "I came along that road two days ago on my way here. It's well above the surrounding farmland. We'd have a head start."

20

"There's a good seven furlongs between the villages. I don't have staff. I can't leave here. Looks like you're Acting Chief Engineer for a little while."

It felt good to be back under discipline. " Materials – what have I got?"

"Blue clay from a pit a mile away. Sand, bags and shovels, as many squaddies as I can commandeer and a contingent of Italian prisoners of war. Don't shout at them – just show them what to do and they'll work."

"How long do I stay"

"God alone knows. Twenty-four hours, two days and nights, a week. The water's rising all over the bloody place, we shall have more than this to worry about before much longer. They say even the Barrier Bank might blow if this weather keeps up. I'll try not to forget you. Just do your best."

He's in charge of the scene, but has no real place in it. A foreigner, as much as the khaki-clad soldiers who obey him, sensing, perhaps resenting, that until recently he was a second lieutenant. The POW's work better, some of them even trying to sing against the wind to give them courage.. Both gangs of men work slowly, steadily and with method. His nose wrinkles at the unfamiliar smells, the blue clay crude and sharp, the sand fusty, smoke from an overturned lantern, exhaust from the straining lorries, the rotten peaty reek of the chewed up land itself. The road surface is disintegrating far too fast, but he's unwilling to stop the lorries just so long as they go on getting supplies through.

Numb feet. The wind an ice-tipped spear straight from the Russian steppes, thrusting up these East Anglian river mouths, shelter from it impossible; like bonfire smoke, it gets you no matter which way you turn. The only certainty is its strength. The bank still holds, intact. All they can do here is continue to work, one team of men filling the sandbags, the other a trudging procession carrying them across the road where each one is added to the wall and fresh clay shovelled up against it. The wind has risen again, singing or speaking are both out of the question.

Another figure looms out of the dark, lantern swinging. "Message just come through – the Wissey bank blew half an hour ago. The water'll be here any minute."

Work, and wait, and wonder how much longer they have. That is all they can do.

Now for a day and a half the water has been rising at five feet an hour, backed by a wind that has veered to the south-west. "Harry," he bellows across to one of the foremen. "Did you check the culverts under the road?"

"Shouldn't worry about them. If she goes, she'll bust over the top, way that wind's blowing."

No time to challenge direct disobedience. Just blind trust. Half a day of warning means they are ahead of the waters and must remain so.

"The road's getting pretty bad," the foreman says. "Better stop them lorries. Dump the clay back there a bit and we'll fetch it, else we'll have a real snarl up. We're nearly run out of bags, too."

"When we do, just shovel the clay on top of the bank."

"Can't do that. See what's happening already." The whole structure, top-heavy, is bulging gently, menacingly, out into the fen. He looks quickly around him for some kind of solution. "Those tarpaulins. Can we weight them, hang them like curtains?"

"Maybe." There's grudging admiration in the foreman's eyes. A calculated risk but they must take it, must act. The bulge grows as they watch. Quickly he gives orders - better a slight overspill to take the level down than a blow out at the toe of the bank where the pressure is so immense. One more thought about the culverts, but no time to let that worry him.

Friday - and his idea has worked. The bank wall is still in one piece. The wind has increased to more than a hundred miles an hour, whipping waves over its top, drenching men and plant alike. No awkward questions about a half bottle of rum a colleague produces. It's welcome, keeps them alive. How good it would be to get back to the Superintendent's house, to have a proper wash and a shave, to sit by the big open fire for a little while. But he gives a tight grin at the foreman who's just suggested it. "No, I'll stay. If I stop, I shan't want to start again. My job's here."

The middle-aged man sitting in the thrumming Engine building, under sentence of death now beyond any doubt, heard the wind scouring across the icy fields, felt the pressure of water all around him. Before very long the elements of wind and water would have had their way and his fragile little brick shelter would be broken and scattered across the fens, and he with it. Trying to stop the water breaking out was his job. He and one of his workmen were on duty, but Bert, simple-minded at the best of times, was busy catching imaginary mice in the sandbags with an old broom. "Much bloody good you are," he thought to himself. One of the great Allen diesels was running though both main drain and river were full to capacity. The other engine was silent, greased and slung up in the metal girders framing the building. It might survive if he didn't. He was sick at heart for the fate of the land he loved. He ached from the cold, from pushing his bike along the rutted track for a mile from the main road, from squelching and slithering in the mud and slub. He took his cap from the nail in the wall, pulled it about his ears and went out on a bank inspection. Nothing, really. A water-rat's hole a few inches from the bank top, right through the core, with a tiny trickle of water coming through. He poked at it with a boot toe, wedging some loose clay back into it, then left it alone and forgot about it. He read his gauges and wrote down the figures, using the collar of his greatcoat as shelter.

A tug and a chain of barges loaded with clay came up river. He went out when he heard the boat's engine, stood on the bank crest to acknowledge the driver with a lifted hand. Suddenly he was aware of the wash, that the rat's hole had re-opened and the water down the bank was a small torrent, coming through with enough force to lift it clear of the ragged brown grass which bound the bank surface, pushing little pellets of clay through, enlarging moment by moment. Then he understood what could happen, and was afraid.

Back inside he went round with an oil can, ate his sandwiches, clearing a small space at the stained table where the tools were kept in neat racks. In sloping meticulous writing he added 'We are just keeping the waters in check in the fens' The river at midnight stood higher than he'd ever recorded, 18'6" above sea level. Six inches – that was all the leeway he had before it came over the bank. 'Today we cemented the doors at the Cam Engine, in case the bank gives way.' Feeling disloyal he wrote again 'We have been abandoned by the River Board, but have organised ourselves and will fight the water to the end.' He re-packed his dockey bag. In that short interval the blowhole had enlarged, the water streaming out with such force that it was hitting the wall of the building, going up and over the roof. He was inside the flood already. He had no telephone, so deep in the fen His family would never know how the end came. Best that way.

"Acting Chief Engineer!" The young man is bitter now it's over. "They gave me the job and I let them down." His head echoes with the explosive triumphant roar of the water as, early on Saturday morning, nudging aside the plug in one of the culverts it hurled itself into the yielding fen, clawing a hole in the road that made a joke of all their efforts, spewing up sandbags and scattering brickwork like confetti. They stood like stone figures as they heard it, complete disbelief on their faces; a shovel half raised, a sentence stopped midway, one of the drivers partly in, partly out of his cab. But they had been winning ...!

Southery Road breach: courtesy Rotary Club of Ely]

Then "Christ Almighty – the bank's gone!" They ran to the scene, or as close to the great jagged gap as they dared go, for the edges of the road were crumbling as the torrent ripped at them. Already the force of the plunging water had torn away one corner of a nearby farmhouse, leaving the bay window framework swinging loose, a net curtain streaming in the wind, and as they stood helplessly watching, the rest of the building disintegrated, a great crack running down from chimney stack to side door as the entire front portion crashed into the furious maelstrom below it.

"You're not responsible" the Superintendent's daughter reassures him. Together they gaze over the flooded fields.

"I am. I should have checked those culverts, gone down personally and looked at them," he retorts. "When the wind changed direction."

Before he can torture himself further with what he should have done, she asks, "Have you got access to a vehicle of any sort?"

"Yes, my old jeep is still just about working. Why?"

"Go down to the Cam Engine. Get Daddy. Something tells me he's in danger, that he needs help."

The Superintendent was almost at the end of his strength. He went to the high-silled door, opened it and glanced around. A cloudless sky bright with stars, the wind still as vicious. Bert was asleep on the sandbags, in a happy land full of real mice. Cruel to wake him. A funny old situation, that the water and the land , the job he loved, would likely be his death. Bricks, mortar, people too – they could only stand so much punishment. He looked towards Dimmock's Cote bridge, where some of the stars were almost big enough to be approaching headlights. No – he was imagining. With so many other crises on hand, who would bother to come and check on one lone drainage superintendent? No-one he knew could get their hands on a vehicle, anyway.

He closed the door. The water pouring over the roof was a dull roar. He'd always loved the stars, and he thought he would try to keep the picture of a star in his mind until he was swept away. After that nothing would matter.

* * * *

That was an attempt to portray a situation. Perhaps I allowed my imagination to run off with me a little But the facts are there, and they are incontrovertible. In the fens, 71,000 acres were under water; thousands of acres of winter wheat and 20,000 tons of potatoes were lost. Houses were destroyed, farms scoured of their fertile soil and hence the farmer's living. One man took a rowing boat and rowed clear through his flooded house, in through the bedroom window at the front and out through the back, so deep was the water in Haddenham fen. The wind blew so violently on the nights of March 16th and 17th that men working on the banks could not stand upright, but had to crawl. When the bank of the Old West River breached, it was estimated that the fen was at one point carrying 70,000,000 tons of water. James Wentworth Day, in his *History of the Fens* to which I am indebted, puts very strongly the case that the Authorities, the Planners, were responsible and stand accused. Rather like today's QANGOS, they were frequently groups of men who had never farmed in their lives, who were given Governmental license to tell farmers what to do and, if they refused, to throw them off their land. In the years after World War 2 these 'Authorities' continued to deepen the channels leading water into the fen basin from the uplands, but made no corresponding improvements to where the water would go once it reached there. And of course no-one anticipated the winter, the Villain Winter as it was subsequently called, when even the sea froze, when whole trains vanished under the snow and up in the hills hung tons of frozen moisture simply waiting the thaw. As Wentworth Day puts it: 'Not a man or a woman gave up. None lost heart. That is the Fen philosophy. At the end of it all, the farmers went back to their scoured-out fields, their dykes full of sludge, their sagging barns, drowned hens and sodden stacks. Cottagers returned to a foot of slime in kitchen and parlour, furniture ruined or floated away, a building with cracking walls or walls that had collapsed. Within a year or less it was all re-built. Today the land grows crops again, and the dykes are clean.'

"MILE AFTER MILE OF BLACK DAMN-ALL"

The Fens are one of those parts of England that you either love or hate. There are no half measures. If they seem, from the previous section, a grim place to be a child, it is not the case. There is an excitement in something monochrome, black and white, a negative in the developing tray. The winters are bitter, open to a scouring east wind that pushes in over the North Sea straight from Russia, a wind that goes through you, not round you. By mid-February there will almost certainly have been some rise and fall in the water level, some inundation of the wash-land, and what Rupert Brooke so perfectly calls 'the thrilling sweet and rotten/Unforgettable, unforgotten river smell' comes to your nostrils. Still little colour, except for the dawns and the incredible winter sunsets, perhaps a chain of geese superimposed against every shade of red and orange that the eye can imagine. Celery stands in ridged-up lines in the fields still, and the winter wheat is beginning to prick through the black soil.

Suddenly, with the winds of March, may come disaster. Fine black peat soil soaks up water readily, but dries up just as quickly. A crust may form across a field, and a gust from the March wind can roll up an entire field into a cloud, together with the precious seeds it contains, and dump it in a field next-door, or fill a carefully dug waterway. Traffic slows to a halt – it is worse than fog, because the windscreen wipers can't dispose of the dust. It simply becomes a fine black mud. It gets everywhere, even when doors and windows are sealed against it. Into wardrobes and cupboards, along the edges of windows, under doors and so across whole rooms. Farmers may have sown sugar-beet, only to harvest their neighbour's wind-sown carrots. In recent years these 'blows' have become less severe, but they are still a threat.

'And after April, when May follows …' Then the Fens begin to dress for the occasion. Ditches fill with celandines, bright as a licked gold coin and so thick they seem to have been painted on with a wide brush. Blackthorn bursts over with creamy froth. In the drains – the large waterways which deliver water to the pumping engines - brandybottle waterlillies send up their first pads. The willow trees haze over with green, and sometimes depending on the type with slender gold catkins. All the cereal crops are now up and flourishing, and the sugar-beet is a dark emerald. Along the edges of the river yellow flag-iris, water forget-me-not, water mint with its pungent muddy overtone, flowering rush and everywhere sheep's parsley, or ladies lace if you prefer the prettier title. Orchards burst into eiderdowns of blossom, lilacs open in the gardens, buttercups dazzle along the banks. It is like watching that waiting negative take on colour, a pattern which carries through until the teazles and huge thistles come, and the land takes on a baked creaminess with the ripening wheat. And so the long slow cycle comes round again, the harvest and the sowing.

Having your soil blow away or flood is not the only hazard in the Fens. The soil can catch fire. Peat fires happen in summer, and can be started by burning off the grass on the side of a ditch or a bonfire of unwanted straw in a field corner. The sour smell of burning peat used often to occur in the days when steam trains ran across the line from Cambridge to Ely. If the fire was on the railway side of the wire fence, father didn't have to worry about it, but if it showed signs of spreading under the wire he'd have his men dig a break, or even divert water from a nearby ditch to damp it down. A peat fire can be dangerous, too. It can burn underground, and to have what you thought was solid ground abruptly disintegrate under your feet, leaving you up to your ankles in warm ashes, is not a pleasant experience. Such fires have been known to burn for years, often following the course of a droveway, only stopping when they come to a watercourse. If they encounter a black bog-oak in their run, they can be almost impossible to put out. Even snow or rain will only damp them down, and as soon as the soil dries out again, the fire takes on new life. One of the few successful ways of dealing with a peat fire is to dig a trench all round the burning area and flood it with water, thus containing it. Pouring water on top of it simply causes an explosion of dust and ashes, then the soil cakes and the fire burrows away under the waterlogged crust.

But there is nothing to equal a walk on a summer evening along a black fen droveway, its surface bound into tapestry with silverweed and wild camomile, the reeds sighing and shivering in the ditches on either side and the slow rustle of a breeze in the ripening wheat.

ENGINE HOUSE DAYS AT STRETHAM

"Run up the Engine and see if your father's on his way home – the Yorkshire pudding will be ruined, again!"

How many Sundays was I asked to do that, when it reached about quarter to two and there was still no sign of father. I used to ask mother, when I grew a bit older, why she couldn't re-arrange dinner time so that it was ready to serve at about 2.00 o'clock, but her irreversible logic was that if she did so, father would come home at 1.00 o'clock and ask why dinner wasn't ready. So father stayed in the Chequers or the Sun, up in the village, until at least half past one before he started to cycle the mile down Green End Road to Engine House. And from the top floor of the beam engine, I could easily see the whole of that road and who was, or wasn't, moving on it.

If I make father sound a real old soak, that is not the case. Saturday you'd been working until midday, so before you went home, still in your working clothes you popped into the pub for a quick one, or two, no more. You needed your lunch, you'd been out round the district since eight o'clock, and you had things to do at home, especially if there was any chance of getting into your own garden. So you didn't linger. But Sunday - well, breakfast was at the unheard-of late hour of nine o'clock, and by the time you'd shaved and fiddled round a bit finding things to do, it was time for the traditional "'Well, I'm just off up to the village," followed by mother's equally traditional request not to be late. And once propping up the bar, you didn't drink that much, but you talked. How you talked. Away from wife and family, with your mates, you settled all the affairs of the village, starting with the church, perhaps, and then the sports teams and the Parish Council. After that you went on to the affairs of the county, the country and finally the world before you realised what the time was. The village wives once got together and bought a clock for the Tap Room at the Sun, which was notorious for stretching its opening hours and keeping many a family waiting for lunch. But the clock didn't last very long. Someone was horsing about and put a dart right through the clock's glass front. Which, as my father remarked with a degree of satisfaction, was the end of that little game.

Being told to run up the engine meant first of all looking up at the nail in the porch to see if the boiler house door was open. The key to that was on a rectangular block of wood, heavy enough to keep it floating should it by chance be dropped into any of the various waterways surrounding the engine buildings. There was the river out front, the main drain at the back, the inlet to the scoopwheel, and the huge concrete cooling tank from which water was circulated to keep the Mirlees diesel engine functioning.

My search for father seems as elusive as the thread of this story. Assuming the key was not there, it meant that the little door to the boiler house was open. So in I went. The cobblestone floor was painful under my shoe soles, being designed for men with hobnailed boots. Three great lancashire boilers faced me, each in its dusty grey asbestos cladding. A ladder with broad plank steps and a handrail gave access to the tops of the boilers so that valves and other mechanisms could be adjusted at need. A metal bar which stood just proud of the cobbles stopped any risk of the ladder sliding backwards. In the corner under the window was a collection of scythes and shearing equipment. I use that word without stopping to think that many people wouldn't know what it meant, might even wonder where sheep came into it. There were similarities. The banks of the main drain and its smaller tributaries were in need of a cut-back at least twice a year. [insert description from letters] and there was also a fearsome device like a chain-saw with two handles, wide enough to stretch across the main drain, which was used by a couple of men, one each side, to cut the waterweed that so much impeded pumping operations. All these I was strictly forbidden to touch. "Them scythes could take your finger off, just like that!" I was told by one of father's workmen. "You come away from 'em, there's a good girl."

Our bikes had specific places where they stood. Mine rested against the sawing horse, an area which always smelled more of freshly cut wood than of oil and coal-dust. Father's bike leant against the tool chest and mother parked hers at the edge of the brick enclosure surrounding the biggest of the boilers which had been converted to hold diesel oil. In later years the jeep, and subsequently the Land rover, stood proud in the centre of the boiler house.

The jeep! That was something else. It came straight from war surplus, and my father maintained that it had desert sand in some of its crevices. It had been converted to protect from the English weather with a roof of curved metal instead of just a windshield, and there were fascinating handles and knobs all over it - for the soldiers to lift it out of sand dunes, I was told. It had four seats sideways on in its open back and in those days there was no regulation to stop children riding in it, so during the school holidays I would often accompany father round the district sitting in the back of the jeep, with a school friend perhaps. Sometimes there would also be a bundle of tools, or a barrel of fuel for the dragline, depending on where we were going.

In those days we really did have buses. Lots of them. The 125a served St Ives and Ely Rail Station. The 121 went to Aldreth, and there was a 137A which went between Ely and Cottenham but only on Thursday Market Day. The 109 was an hourly service between Cambridge and Ely, and I could see it coming along the Cambridge Road as I pedalled furiously up Green End, knowing that the two stops in the village before the central one would give me just enough extra time to put my bike away and dash for the stop. There were specific places in the village where people could leave their bikes without thinking of chaining or locking them. The Post Office yard was one, on the High Street and convenient for bus stops. Some people left their bikes in one of the livery rooms at the Rectory, empty now that there were no longer horses in the stable. Even when father and I cycled into Ely on an occasional summer Saturday, my legs flying round to keep up with his steady pedalling, we left our bikes unlocked in the outbuildings of one of the pubs, knowing that they would be there when it was time for home.

So I'm opening the door into the main engine building. I would like to say that the majesty and might of the huge beam engine that met my eye when I pushed it open impressed me each time that I saw it. But it would not be true. With the child's ability to find every-day things quite normal, I simply ran up the three flights of stairs to the top landing and the window from which I could do my look-out job. The huge beam, 50ft long, each of its two panels cast in a single piece, the shining, constantly greased piston rod, the huge cylinder, the connecting rod to the fly-wheel, all these were part of my life. The sandbags stored on the cylinder landing were no more than somewhere I could climb. The oddities on the windowsills of the top landing, deer-antler picks used by Neolithic men and the vertebra from a pterodactyl which the shrinking peat had revealed, tools such as a becket, a wooden shovel with a metal angle at its base for cutting turf, a threshing flail, its three-dimensional join fastened with a dried eel-skin, these were part of life, something to be touched as one went past in a kind of rhythm. Stranger things than that lay around me. Somewhere in a museum there is a fossil plesiosaurus minus one of its tail bones – because that tail bone is on my windowsill. The matchbox on the mantelshelf in the study held Roman coins from a pot which the dragline had struck and broken open. In the bureau a superb flint axe-head and a massive core-tool. Even in the village my school-friends had to learn about such things from books. I had the reality within my grasp.

And the reality was a little black dot on the road from the village. Ten minutes unless it was a head wind, that was all it took. So I could scuttle back down the dusty steps again, shut and lock the doors and thunder down the passage at the side of the house. "He's on his way, Mum! You can make the gravy." My own special last-minute job was to use the water pump just outside the back door, which fed from an underground spring running through a gravel bed several feet under the bed of the river. After a few moments of pumping away the standing water, what came out was chill enough, even on a warm July day, to frost the glass of the big pink water jug.

We were "the Fen Kids" and from that definition you would have thought that we had fins, yellow bellies and vestigial tails. The small group of us who lived on Stowbridge Farm just over the wooden bridge were only just Fen Kids. There were others who subsequently joined us in that row of five houses who had come from deeper in the Fen and had some strange habits. I remember going out to speak to the two brothers who had newly come up from Further Farm, down by the Cam Engine, and finding one of them quite happily munching chickweed from the bank. They also had strange names for things. A branch with a V-shape at the end was a Dig-a-ditch, and any farm machinery was a Ning-a-ning, taken I think from the noise made by the flywheel on the old John Deere tractor which their father drove.

The first house you came to as you approached the bridge was Jack Day's. He was the foreman of the farm, which was at that time part of Fred Hiams' Estates. His daughter Christine didn't ride to school with us, as her father had a car and took her to the village in it. Somehow the river was a barrier between her and the rest of us, indefinable but a fact all the same. Once over the river, you could consider yourself on the farm.

To give some idea of our activities, I need to describe the layout of the five farms that made up our part of Hiams' Estates. They were laid out in a rough kind of hexagon. We all lived at Stowbridge Farm, though as the Drainage Superintendent's daughter I was a kind of hybrid, neither fish nor flesh. Over the bridge the roads divided, my road home going to the left, and one of the main droves going off to the right along the base of the river bank. Follow that drove along a dog's-hind-leg pattern and you'd reach the concrete road. Turn right down that and you'd come to Chittering Farm. Turn left and there were two possibilities. The concrete road led to Box Farm, so called because there was a railway signal box there. But before you reached that, you could take Cross Drove which would bring you out just short of the third farm, Fidwell where the herd of Frisian Cows was kept, and that drove led back to Stowbridge. Often in the early summer, before it was deemed warm enough to spend the evening in the river, one of the boys would say 'Coming for a run?' and off we'd go. Past Long Sheds, on to the concrete road and up to Cross Drove, not choosing to run on the ribbed concrete but on the soft dusty edge where the soil bounced slightly under our feet. On Cross Drove there was a deep ditch and on a quiet evening you could hear the drinker moth caterpillars, big pursy creatures with spiky orange fur – chewing their way through the reeds that lined it. Or a sedge warbler, a bird so small you could have held it in your closed fist, would begin to chitter at us because we'd unintentionally come too close to her nest. Past The Bear Tree, an old willow which had lost three of its branches at various times and had three broken layers rather like steps, hence its connection with the three bears of the nursery rhyme. Tiring, now, and our feet beginning to ache, so we ran thirty paces and walked thirty paces. We'd plunge into the reed-bed, grab a stem, unfurl its central spathe and pull out the innermost section, then if you blew hard a kind of whistle could be made. So back over the 9ft Drain, one of the feeders to Main Drain, across past the pigsties so we could rattle a stick along their boundary fence and shout 'Pig, pig, pig!' making the inhabitants run round and round and squeal, down the path past all the willows and perhaps up into our den in the gable roof of the gig shed, if it wasn't too late. We could see our parents calling us, but I don't think anyone ever knew about that hidey-hole.

Cruger Gillett, who lived in the first house over the bridge, was the pig man on the farm. We used to be-devil him round the pig shed, where he boiled surplus potatoes from the fields for the saddle-back pigs the farm reared. We'd wait outside the shed, which had two doors and always smelt of meal and steam, until he'd gone off on his rounds with the pig-swill in a kind of enormous barrow, then we'd dive in the other door and grab potatoes from the deep trough in the concrete floor where they were tipped when cooked to cool off. Yes, they were dirty on the outside but inside they were hot and tasty as we broke them open. Then suddenly a shout from one of us. "Look out - Cruger's coming back!" We'd scatter, while he broke into a run to try and catch us, calling us Young Buggers and threatening to tell our parents. That he never did so seems to me now an indication that he really quite enjoyed the game.

Next door to him was a pair of semi-detached houses where when I was young lived one of the field workmen and his family, Keith and Maureen, then next to them was Finchy, the dear gentle old horsekeeper and his wife who were always welcoming to a child with not much to do. Horses, you think to yourself – how far back in time are we travelling with this story? Surely that kind of thing belongs with the mother, not the daughter. Not a bit of it. Percheron.horses were bred at Stowbridge Farm, and still used when I was young to draw carts, to pull the cutter-binder and sometimes to plough. The breed originates in La Perche, in France, as a very smart type of carriage horse. Subsequently their lack of fetlocks, the thick hair around the feet, made them popular for farm work. They were medium sized, jet black when foaled. The working horses were dapple grey with white manes. As they reached old age they became white. I was very small indeed when my father first taught me how to offer grass to a horse from the other side of the wire fence – flat on your palm, not held out in a bunch which would possibly mean a nasty bite, the horse being unable to tell grass from fingers.

One day, a working mare ran mad. It was high summer, hot and thundery, and perhaps she had been bitten once too often by a horse fly. Whatever the reason, they backed her up to the loading bay and tipped the cart to unload it. When it was in position again, and her driver gave her the word "Wuch-up, me old gal" to start her, the cart went through a dip in the drove way and all the harness rattled. That set her off – she threw her driver with one huge upward rear and came pounding along the drove, the cart rattling and banging more and more the faster she galloped. My mother rushed out to get me where I was playing in the road and dragged me under the fence of the garden belonging to the cottage next door – only just in time. I can still hear the thudding hooves and the snorts of the terrified mare as she went full pelt for her stable, to be rid of this thing behind her. By this time, fortunately, she had almost winded herself. They'd called the old horsekeeper from his house, though he was retired, because she'd been a foal in his care, and when he addressed her by her own name she pulled to a stop, sides heaving, mouth flecked with foam. "Whoa, Dolly, whoa – good girl, easy now". He soothed and calmed her, until she allowed him to detach the harness holding the cart to her and lead her into the stable yard. The workmen, including the driver who had not been more than bruised in his fall, muttered amongst themselves that she'd not have answered to any other man on the farm.

Accidents happened in winter too. The LNER main line to Kings Lynn ran across the fen at the back of Engine House. The men used the trains to tell the time. "Here come the 11.00 o'clock – time for dockey," and out would come the canvas bags, the sandwiches and the flasks. There were several unmanned crossings over this line. One foggy November day a team made up of a farm worker called Towser Barber leading a horse with an empty cart, to the back of which was tethered another horse being taken back to the stables, moved down the drove towards the railway. The man tethered his horse to the fence, opened the gate and stood listening carefully for any sound in the rails which would indicate the approach of a train, as he could see no more than a few feet either way. Hearing nothing, he unhitched the horse and began to lead the little cortege across the line. The train which smashed into them snapped the harness as if it was cobwebs, so Towser said afterwards, and carried the empty cart half a mile down the track. But miraculously, neither he nor the two horses received a scratch. It would be great to think that Towser attributed his survival to the Almighty, but in fact the engine driver was just beginning to slow up for the rise to Iron Bridge over the Old West River, which probably saved his life.

Next door to our house was the Stoker's Cottage, where I spent the first 18 months of my life. Dann'l Vail and his wife Joan, with their son Peter lived there. Peter would often come toddling round to Engine House and as the back door was always open, into the kitchen. He was about two years younger than me. On one occasion mother was preparing horseradish for pickling in vinegar, and Peter picked up a chunk of the bare root from the table. 'Not 'ot,' he said and bit off a piece. Did he yell! His mother came rushing round thinking that he'd been murdered at the very least, but when she learned the truth she could only laugh.

I had to be diplomatic as I grew older as to who I played with. Joan Vail and Annie Bond were both part of the team of women who worked on the land, singling sugar beet and picking up potatoes. They were either bosom friends or desperate enemies, and their sons followed whatever was the order of the day. So at the start of a week I could be playing happily with Michael and

Robert Bond, only to have them told not to speak to me because I'd also played with Peter. By the end of the week the whole situation could have reversed itself.

During the summer holidays – harvest holidays as they were still called – we all got together and went over to Ebb Everitt's orchards in Wilburton to pick plums and apples. At least, our mothers did. We kids had no option but to go along, starting with the early morning bike ride. That was one thing my mother was allowed to do, though singling sugar beet was considered 'below her' and I used to enjoy my days in the orchards. We were under some constraints, of course. We were never to pick any fruit from any tree, and if we were caught climbing a ladder Mr. Everitt threatened us with a hiding. But any fruit that had fallen was ours to pick and gnaw at, ripe or not. The first plums were, I think, Rivers. Small, blue-red fruit. Then came Czars, bigger and of a dark maroon colour. The main crop was Victorias, golden yellow one side, red the other as the sun had shone on them. A few trays of greengages were harvested, and the plum season ended with big golden egg and special named varieties for which the orchards were well-known, fruit that went straight to the jam factories rather than local markets. By that time, the middle of August, Ellisons apples and the first Worcesters were ripening. We were chased by wasps, covered with dust, sticky with fruit juice and exhausted by climbing in the lower branches of the young trees by knocking-off time at 3.00 p.m. So back on our bikes and swooping round our mothers, being told 'Look out – keep on the path, you'll get yourself run over' we made our way home and our weary mothers went straight into cooking the evening meal for husbands due home by half past four.

I owe a great deal to my father, because he taught me to, as he put it, think with my feet and see with my fingers. Although as I have said he often went up to the village on a Sunday for a pint or two, there were other Sundays when he had to go and open a sluice at the behest of one of the local farmers, or perhaps shut one down if there had been a lot of rain. 'Coming up the bank?' he'd say, and before he'd been into the boiler house to get the sluice key, I'd have my boots and coat on and be ready.

He knew a lot about flowers, birds and bees. There were one or two particular places that we visited at a certain time of year to see specific flowers. He always knew where the best pussy-willow trees were to be found, or where there would be a ditch enamelled with celandines. In May, we'd go up into the fields beyond Berry Green in Stretham, where cowslips grew and among them a little dark purple orchid, I think it is known as the burnt orchid. We'd pick cowslips and take them home for cowslip tea, pale gold and delicate. He'd take care to tell me when the Marsh Marigolds came into bloom, a massive curve of deep gold in the inlet between Jack Day's wash and the one next to it, and then we'd go for a walk along that bank so we could look more closely at them. One particular field, an uncultivated corner between the Old West and the LNER railway, was called Dog Daisy field because the wild ox-eye daisies grew there, and that had to visited. We would sometimes combine it with a trip to the Fish and Duck pub as it would be summer. In late August if we were visiting Tile House Farm to open the sluice up there, he'd straddle the ditch alongside Mr. Hazel's field and find the first ripe dewberries. The game was 'One for you, and one for me, and one for the stranger' and somehow the stranger always seemed to be me!

The final surprise of the year was late in September. On our bikes, we'd go down to 'The Pits' which were the quarries left in the loose limestone, called clunch, from which the foundations of the Dimmocks Cote bridge over the Cam had been dug. There were three, if I remember. One of them was still in use, though not a great deal. New surfaces were constantly being exposed, and it was full of fossils – nothing spectacular, but there were pieces of ammonite, and shells. In the base of the pit was a shallow lake with a colony of Great Crested Newts. The second pit, next to the road, was strictly forbidden. It had been filled to half level with some kind of acidic industrial waste which with the slightest breeze caught at your nostrils. It had burned all the foliage brown, and killed the trees so that they stood out like black skeletons. It had been 'dinned into us' as we said about something repeated and repeated, not to go anywhere near that pit, as if we fell in we'd be burnt to death, and knowing the casual way in which they left such substances around in those days, it is quite likely that whatever was in the pit was pretty lethal. We certainly didn't try to get close.

The third pit was up a drove, and ended at a tumbledown cottage where I think the Foreman of the clunch diggers lived while they were excavating. Through the pit ran a little watercourse where they'd bring shallow barges to get the stone down to the river itself. But the thing we went to see was an autumn spectacular, a guelder rose tree, which before it lost its leaves, turned them a deep scarlet and also decked itself with clusters of red berries, almost luminous in the rays of the setting sun. It was so totally different from any other tree in the fens that it didn't seem at all strange we should go and make pilgrimage to it just once a year.

Father also showed me how to make a poppy lady. You need a strong field poppy, which has only been out a little while. You must gently coax the petals back from the central pistil, without pulling them off. You tie them with a sash of a grass blade, then rub off half the black stamens so that those left look like black hair. Break off a stem of grass and thread it through the 'dress' you have made to look like arms, and add one more piece of poppy stalk for a second 'leg'.

I must tell a little about going to see Mr. Hazell. The family lived at Tile House Farm, which had been a place where retiring Roman Legionaries and soldiers used to stop over. It was on the edge of what had been a shallow mere, but there was a gravel-bottom ferry over the river and a track leading up towards Akeman Street when it was time for them to take to the road again. Following drainage of the Mere, a large service of Roman pewter dishes and plates, with glass bottles and other ware, was found on its edge and a horde of the last types of Roman coin to reach Britain was recovered from the same area. Ploughing and harrowing would continually bring up chunks of Roman tile and pottery, which had given the farm its name, not – as some people thought – because the house was tiled. They were a very individual family. I think that one of them had managed to 'escape' and marry, but the others all still lived at the farm with their mother, though they were men and women in their 40's and 50's. On a typical Sunday, Mr. Percy and Miss Marion would have gone up to the Baptist chapel, leaving Mr. Reg to look to the animals. The other children were all deaf mutes. Mr Archie and Miss Mary were quite capable of making expressive noises, and had their deafness been attended to no doubt would have spoken quite normally. Mr. Albert was a true deaf mute, never so much as a grunt from him. Miss Mary did exquisite needlework and crochet, and both she and Mr. Archie had learned to read the newspaper, which seems amazing to me even now. Mr. Reg used to take me to see a new calf or foal if there was one, or let me help hunt for eggs round the stackyard, and then he and father would have a gossip about the land. A bundle of Farmers Weekly magazines would be tied with string and given to me to carry home. One day the Old Lady expressed a wish to see me. She had not altered her habits since she became a widow, rather like Queen Victoria, and I was ushered into her presence where she sat in the front parlour, in a round velvet chair with her feet on a little velvet hassock. She was wearing a long black dress and had a white lace cap on her head. I think that I believed she was Queen Victoria for a little while. She spoke graciously to me, asking if I was a good girl. I was quite dumbfounded and soon backed away from this matriarch, biting my lip.

Rumour had it that, the Hazels being a very rich family, they were going to be the first ones ever to take it all with them when they died. Certainly, one of their distant relations, a Miss Jewell, lived alone in a huge Georgian house along Wilburton Road in Stretham and could have had almost unlimited wealth at her command. But she was one of those strange reclusive women often found in a small community. She lived entirely in her kitchen with an enormous flock of cats, ate potatoes from the saucepan she had cooked them in using a newspaper on one corner of the table as a tablecloth. She wore a print wrapper round her ample form, and I think I remember her having at least one mole on her face with several gray hairs growing from it. She was very kind to us children. Village women whispered among themselves about a tragedy in her life – perhaps she was one of those girls nominally 'widowed' by the Great War. What treasures might have been secreted in other rooms of that house we never found out, because no-one ever got further than her kitchen.

Earlier in this narrative I mentioned having a dinosaur bone on my windowsill. It was father's keen eye which identified the fossilised skeleton of a plesiosaurus over 30ft long in the gault pit on the Wicken Road. He'd been yarning with the foreman who was in charge of a gang topping up the banks with clay, and father happened to notice some odd-looking bones when one lorry shot its load down. He picked one up, and said to the Foreman 'You'd better call a halt, I think. You've got something there.' At least, that was what he told us. I know that the dinosaur was revealed, lying on a newly cut shelf of clay, and was declared to be between 130 and 150 million years old. We school children went down in procession to see it, where it was roped off and guarded by Mr. Lythell, the village policeman, leaning portentously on his bicycle. It subsequently went into the Sidgwick Geological Museum in Cambridge, minus one tail bone which had somehow found its way into father's pocket. When father died, I asked a family member if I should admit to this 'abstraction' on his part. 'Lord, no' came the answer, in his best Varsity drawl, 'they'd probably ask you if you wanted the whole animal back.' So I kept quiet.

ROUND AND ROUND THE GARDEN

Which, of course, is impossible as the garden at Engine House was square, a continuation of the L-shape that the house itself made. It was bounded on two sides by a thick hawthorn hedge and at the bottom was a fence of iron railings. Thrushes and blackbirds nested in the hedge every spring, secure from the cats that roamed the yard. There was a horde of them, with a distinct order of precedence. Sooty, the black matriarch, went through the porch and scullery and into the kitchen as and when she chose. Others who tried that were met with a snarl, a spit and a flashing paw. My grandmother who spent her last years living with us used to buy cheap sliced bread and an extra pint of milk from her pension to feed her cats, and I am convinced that they heard the moment she put on her shoes in her bedroom in the morning, because suddenly the garden would thicken with cats the way a sauce thickens on the stove. I think we had something like thirteen of them at once point. She was also merciless in finding and drowning their endless litters of kittens, dreadful as it seems to us in these days. Had she not been so vigilant we would have been totally over-run. When she 'dined down' at weekends Jo, the favourite of all the cats, would climb on the back of her chair and walk backwards and forwards, to be greeted by 'Wer, you old fool you!' and a morsel of meat that she had learned to take gracefully from fingers.

In the hedge corner was a huge walnut tree, at its foot, most mysterious to a child, a clump of ferns which vanished each autumn and re-appeared in spring, uncurling as the days grew longer and lighter. I was very young indeed when I first showed an interest in gardening. We had evacuees staying with us and I had found a large worm that I wanted to show to one of them. Picture it - a terrified boy of fourteen or so trying to escape a determined toddler, yelling to my mother "'Ere, missus, get 'er orff me - she's got a bleeding great snake!"

My father grew roses. There had always been roses in the garden, some of them very old bushes that had been planted there in the days before that house was built, when another house occupied its site. Roses which, perhaps, collectors would these days have enthused over. In the L-shape itself was a squatty, slender stemmed bush which never grew more than about four feet high and needed little pruning. It budded by the end of April and was in bloom by May, carrying its small double petalled pink cups through the summer and into October. I rooted a cutting and was able to lay some of its blossoms on my mother's coffin many years later. In the rose garden at Warwick Castle I found it growing as a specimen, with a label saying it was Old China. Outside the porch was a trellis bearing a single red rambler that smelled pungently of fish-paste, and near it a rampant couple of bushes rich with small double white flowers that had no perfume at all but glowed with a kind of luminescence on summer nights. Where the hedge began by the lounge windows was a very strange yellow moss-rose, its stems thick with fine prickles, its small blossoms smelling of lemon-curd. Down in the vegetable garden was a standard Frau Carl Druschki, buds streaked with deep carmine feathering but opening to a whiteness past that of snow, the petals thick and textured like blotting paper. Summer had arrived when Frau Carl opened her first blossom, for she was a choosy flower and didn't come out until she was sure of the climate.

When I was about twelve, my father discovered Wheatcrofts rose catalogue, which in those days when glossy magazines were few and far between was a treat simply to open and read. By then his salary had increased to a degree that he could think of buying some of the wonderful things that we all three pored over at night in the winter months. He insisted on having the new rose Peace planted by the gate. When I asked why, he simply said, "Peace be to this house, and to all that dwell therein," which, later, I discovered in the Book of Common Prayer. But next to her was Tzigane, the gipsy, petals streaked in red and orange disarray, which perhaps was a clue to the other side of the man who had chosen her. Queen Elizabeth, Superstar, Soraya, Blue Moon, he had them all.

There were curious things all round that garden. Lilies of many kinds. Madonnas, with their golden pollen to stain my nose when I sniffed at them. Regale lilies filling the summer evenings with the smell of vanilla fudge. I must have been very small when my mother first told me the story of the Crown Imperial lily, 'Angels Tears' as she called it. There was a big clump of them by the middle path and I can see her now squatting down to lift one of the bells, very gently so as not to snap its stem, and showing me the dimple at the top of each petal with its 'tear' of sap. Saying that once it had been a proud flower with its head raised high and open to the sun. But on Good Friday it was the only flower that would not bend its head when Jesus passed on his way to Calvary. So an angel was sent down to bend the flower's stubborn head for it, and learning why, the flower wept, tears it has carried from that day to this. Botanically impossible, yes of course, but what a wonderful way to interest a child in a flower.

Jasmine flourished in that garden, yellow in a great billowing hooped skirt all round the shed window, white on a mesh arch across a connecting path. Like Frau Carl, the opening of the white jasmine meant summer had arrived and distant aunts from London, receiving a postcard to that effect, would make pilgrimage to come and smell it. I have never found a distiller or perfume-maker who can exactly reproduce that smell; always it turns to soap in the nostrils whereas the living flower has an unmistakable acid tang behind its sweetness.

Fruit we had in abundance. An absolutely huge rhubarb patch was watched keenly as April became May, for the first pies and crumbles. So big were the leaves that we sometimes used them for sun-bonnets on hot days. Father was very keen to spot the first flowers on the rhubarb heads and cut them off, which puzzled me until he explained that if it flowered, the plant would have a bitter taste. Gooseberries came later, a row of them down by the lawn. Watched just as anxiously as June came in. They were not the kind that goes yellow and translucent, and were either made into pies or jam, or preserved in Kilner jars. By late August the Victoria Plum close to the back door brought wasps into the house and made my father's workmen swear when they mowed our lawn because the pips of fallen fruit blunted the scythe blade. Mother used to set a traditional trap for the wasps, a glass jar that had held jam, filled with water, a circle of paper tied down over it with string and a hole poked in that paper with the end of a pencil. The wasps would alight on the rim, start to sip the sweet water, loose their footing and tumble into the jar where they drowned.

When I was only about six years old, this gave me an idea. That summer there was a wasps nest just the other side of the iron railings at the bottom of the garden, and I thought I would save the wasps the journey to the scullery. So I took the jar of water and dead wasps, when mother wasn't looking, trotted down the path and poured it into the entrance hole of the nest. I might have escaped had I not hung around to see what would happen. My mother told me that when I came galloping, shrieking, up the path I was invisible for the wasps that were around me, stinging me everywhere, face, hands, legs. They were inside my clothes and shoes, and even she was badly stung getting me clear of them. All she could do was grab the blue-bag from the windowsill of the washhouse, where she had steered me and my terrible cargo, and rub me all over with it. It was the traditional remedy for a single sting, but an unknown for such a severe attack, but I survived, and after that kept my distance from wasps nests.

We are still only halfway round the garden. Two apple trees had pride of place on the lawn, one a Worcester and one a very old cooking apple producing only a few fruit, each big and mis-shaped with a texture of custard. They were delicious in an apple suet pudding, and if they could be gathered before they decided to fall, which was a rather random matter, they would keep. Another similar cooking apple tree stood at the junction of the path from the back door and the path along the bottom of the garden, its branches half caught up in a great oblong mass of ivy. At the end of the middle path was a Laxtons Supreme which suffered from codlin moth infestation and as we had plenty of apples father didn't bother to ask the men to grease-band it when the females were about. So by August the infested apples had ripened early and were falling in profusion. Good to eat, so long as you avoided the little passage through which the codlin grub had made its exit, to pupate in the soil at the base of the tree.

The outside wall of the lounge carried an enormous espalier pear tree with big, heavy dark green pears that would never ripen on the branches, no matter how good the autumn. They had to be hand picked, wrapped in newspaper and stored in a dark cool cupboard. By Christmas they ripened to a golden perfection, so juicy that the only way to eat them was to cut them in slices with a pen-knife. No-one knew its name. It was just called 'the big pear tree'. My great-grandfather John Sennitt had a similar tree, so my father told me, and once exhibited two kinds of pears at the village produce show. The judges all knew that he had only the one tree, and penalised him for cheating, but he took them to his garden and showed that he had grafted a second kind of pear onto one half of the great tree, so that it bore two kinds of fruit. Uncertain of the ethics of this, it seems the judges awarded him a special prize for ingenuity.

Down the middle path was a small Williams pear. It never seemed to grow very much or produce a great deal, though what it did yield was tasty. A true square peg in a round hole. Next to it a Conference with its long fuzzy textured fruit. But the crown of the collection was a Doyenne de Comice standing near the walnut tree. To reach up and pick one of them, on a warm September evening, to bite deep into it and feel the juice run down my chin was an out-of-self experience.

There were three distinct areas of garden. The vegetable garden was the largest. My father, like most family men in those days, grew all the potatoes we would need for the year and they were put in a clamp during the winter which I was told not to touch on pain of death, though its smooth earthy sides were a great temptation, as was the fan of straw sticking out of its ventilation hole. He also grew leeks, carrots, brussels sprouts for the winter, both white and purple broccoli and in summer, starting them off under high barn cloches, two or three different kinds of lettuce.

We weren't the kind of people who pulled a lettuce into its individual leaves and poured dressing over it. The Cos lettuces, today re-named Romaine, in particular, were father's pride and were cut fresh from the garden for tea, washed at the sink, quartered, then laid in a long glass dish for the table. Because the kitchen floor was quarry tiled, it did no harm to pick up a lettuce quarter and, being careful to hold down the central stem which was oozing its white, bitter, slightly narcotic juice, flick the water out of the leaves on to the floor. We were quite used to doing that. One of my townie boy-friends came to the house, and tried to do as we did but failed to hold on to the stem. Half his lettuce portion snapped off and shot clean through the scullery and out of the back door, disturbing a snoozing cat.

Mother was in charge of the flower garden. a good hand at pruning bushes. She had to be, as there were several in the garden. One of the first things I remember her saying to me was "Don't touch the secateurs!" Forsythia, flowering currant of a particularly foxy smell, a rosy red japonica down beside the huge rhubarb bed, white lilac involving a constant battle against suckers, because it was determined to colonise the whole garden, honeysuckle just outside the back door where the moths purred and hovered on summer nights, orange blossom [as we called it] and deutzia with its little white bells. She grew tulips of all colours, polyanthus, great beds of violets, both blue and white. Later, huge clumps of paeonies, deep mulberry pink in colour. A row of blue cranesbill. A perennial sweet pea, white and prolific, another plant which mystified me to start with by its winter vanishing act. Gladioli as the summer waned into autumn. Perennial sunflowers reproduced themselves with their tubers down by the rhubarb bed and my grandmother, while she could still get around, waged unending war against them. "I'm bin out in the garden and got most of them ole sunflowers up," she'd say with some triumph. These days they sell them in garden centres. She also fought to the death a blue bell-flower, though why she was so against it I never knew. And there was no more determined fighter of twitch grass, as we called it, which needed every bit of its white thread of root removing or it would simply colonise again. Mother's *finale* was chrysanthemums of all kinds, single Korean pink ones which always suffered from autumn rains and flopped to earth, little button ones that stood upright no matter what the weather did and the big shaggy bronze-headed ones which lasted until the frosts felled them. There were window boxes full of geraniums and lobelia and she purloined an area of the vegetable garden for herbs, lemon thyme, a shapely bush of grey sage, spearmint for mint sauce and apple mint for the vegetable saucepans.

I had a garden of my own from an early age so long as I could keep it tidy, under the walnut tree. While I was still in my pram it had been the chicken-run, and there was a large heap of chicken manure just outside it. Somehow I managed to drag at the reins holding me in the pram, wriggle down to the end of it, tip the whole contraption up and was found having a wonderful time smearing chicken mess all over myself. At one end of it was a purple lilac, double flowered and so pungent of scent as to be almost intoxicating especially after a late May shower. But other than that I could grow what I liked. Cress, radishes, cosmos daisies because the seeds were big and easy to plant. I bought a tamarisk tree, an end-of-day bargain on Ely market.. In spite of the soil conditions being almost totally wrong, it flourished and bloomed. Sometimes father would let me have the young lettuces or sprouts he singled out from his own beds, or – treasure of treasures – a tomato plant, and then as I grew more careful, a cloche to put it under.

The men my father employed were also contracted to hoe the paths, trim the hedge and mow the lawn, but there was always work out there and most times, if any of the three of us was missing from the house during the hours of daylight, we'd be in the garden, lopping, tying back, digging and manuring, scrunching an early apple, sometimes just leaning on the handle of a garden fork, relishing the smell of turned earth and admiring what we'd done.

GOING ROUND THE ENGINE

Interior of Stretham Beam Engine]

It is time for my father to speak out once again. This time he is taking a party of visitors round the old beam engine, something that he did increasingly often at weekends as more and more people got to know about it.

' … and when we go next door you will see the Engine didn't just push the water through, it lifted, it was a very scientific force, lifting and squeezing the water then letting it go. I'll try and explain that later when I get you in there.

Now it lifted the water from the fens – because you've already learned that our fens are much lower than the river. So all right. The cost of the engine house was two thousand quid. They all agreed to have this thing built – by "they" I mean my bosses, in 1830 on 29th day of June and this engine house had got to be built by the first week in December. If not there was a £10 per day penalty, and we know from our log books that by January of the next year, 1831, it was actually at work. There were no railways – leastways, not in our fen at that time – so she was obviously shifted by midland canal systems, pitched into flat bottom boats and pulled up here by men, or donkeys. And then they tipped her out onto the washland – the shore, here – and told Charlie to put her up, and Charlie put her up. And we wonder just how many men there were here, where they lived, where they came from. They couldn't live in the village, because even when I was a lad the road down to the Engine was just a green drove, and there was only the wooden bridge. The village would be quite inaccessible. That's enough of that - you mustn't get me on this too much, because otherwise you won't get any lunch today. But now for some points about the old girl herself.

She is 100 HP. When they altered the valves – and I'll tell you about that in a moment – they added another 5HP, but she was 100 HP when built. In my time we used to try and keep her down to 12 revs per minute, sounds strange, doesn't it, 12 rpm, but you see there was no braking system on her, just the weight of the water. The beam – but you don't know how it works yet, do you. I've got in front of myself. It's the simplest engine in the world. Steam pushes the cylinder up, the beam rises, and that connecting rod comes down and it then moves the wheel. That fly-wheel is made of iron, in case you think it's made of wood or concrete, and it has to be as big as that and weight as much as that so as to work. You see, after that crank has done its work, then there would have been one revolution, but with such a great weight she was capable of swinging herself over for the next stroke. All right, so – she's 21 ft centre to centre on the beam, the con-rod is a piece of mathematical precision, I've got a book indoors which shows the weight of these things, not one pound under or over.

I won't tell you any more because otherwise you won't see the engine at all. Now if you stay there, I'll show you how she used to start. [At this point he moved up to cylinder landing where starting handle and gear lever are located, and indicated the steam feed pipe coming through wall.]

Steam came from the boilers next door, right, and er, when you come up here, don't be like the people who come in boats, they take pictures, then they show them to their friends at Christmas time and they write to me, "Dear Mr Clarke, we did enjoy visiting your old engine and, ah, we found it so strange because the steam goes direct to the cylinder" – well of course it doesn't do anything of the sort. It goes into a 6 inch jacket which is all the way round the cylinder. These are the valves; she's a Watt double-acting engine so there are valves top and bottom. Right, so we've got the starting handle. Now the crank would be either this way round or that way round, but that's how he would start. Now up here you may be able to see, this lever, if I push that down she'd come down towards me and I would then push back into neutral and push that one and she'd go up and then you'd pull her back again, and she swings back and up and back, and up again, each time you're trying to get her up an inch, perhaps two inches more. This could take ten minutes, or a lot longer, depending.

When you went through that door, it was an automatic gesture to turn the key. Now they didn't do that because they were afraid anyone would steal their occupation. It was so that nobody would interrupt them. I said to Mr Stevens once – Could I watch you start the engine? And he said – Yes, but stand over there and don't speak to me. Now you'll understand this, you mustn't go high on that con-rod and when she starts to judder you must do that [docs something with lever] or she'll stop, and you don't want her to stop, you've got to keep moving one way or the other. So in the middle of all this performance, say the stoker would stick his head round the door and say "Hoy, so-and-so wants something" and you couldn't have that, so they automatically turned the key in the door.

So you keep swinging her up and up, and eventually she'll come over, then this little lever here, well that takes over the work of the valves and so she is now an engine. Up till then, she'd just been a man-driven machine, hadn't she. Now you may think about the engine driver "Well, he's all right now, he's got nothing to do except sit down and watch things go round." But the engine needs a constant watch on her, she's maybe only doing 3 or 4 rpm so you've got to work her up, and this is the vital bit. I have done this and you've got to push her. Suppose she's coming round at, say, 3 or 4 rpm so what you had to do to get extra speed was, you had to carefully watch her and kid of ease her along.

Now after this engine had been running about ten years, they found they weren't shifting enough water and wondered why. And then, you see, they discovered that the drains had gone well below the level where they'd started, below that little hole in the wall there where I showed you how to see the level of water in the drain, that's the internal bit of the district. Now the river was five feet higher than the land in the fen, at least it was in those days 100 years ago.

Now the water which the scoop wheel delivered was 120 tons per minute, a surprising amount of water when you consider that our very modern diesels can only lift 150 tons. This old girl did a marvellous job; she worked all those years right up to 1925 when the diesel was installed next door. Of course, we don't pump from this engine at all now except for a very small amount – we've got two engines which pump into the Cam, and the district is divided by dams.

Now these Height of river and Height of drain gauges were only installed in 1870. Before that the poor old Superintendent had to rely on his stoker keep a-running round the place looking at the level, so as when he put his head out of the engine room door the stoker could tell him what the levels were. Therefore, you see, the stoker would have to watch the water feed system into the boilers, as well as stoking. Now of course when you stoke a long boiler like this – well, I learned my craft at Upware Engine, and the first time you get a shovel full of coal, you stand too close and Clang, the shovel hits the boiler surround and all the coal tumbles round you on the floor, and your Head Stoker laughs, and maybe the Superintendent himself comes down that flight of stairs to see what the hell's going on. But you need to put one shovel full right down the middle to the back. Have any of you ever seen a man stoking a railway engine, which is something like?

Then you put one shovel full down the left, and one down the right, and so she goes on. Was there a safety valve – well Yes, there was. Once a year someone would sit on this safety valve and blow it off."

Well, that was me taking a party over the old beam engine. Now I shall probably try and tell you more about my life – I don't know who on earth is going to be interested in that, my life as a fen-man. And I shall try and tell you something of what I did. For instance I can remember, naturally I can remember when there were no tractors, when the fens were as quiet as we are now. Just the horses working on the farms, and the men working in gangs or perhaps singly. My word, there were some funny old things happened to me in my time though. Let's see if I can remember one or two of them, while this machine is running.

I remember a real old panic at Upware Engine - that'd be about 1928 when I was just a young man. Suppose, just suppose, you have to stop in a hell of a hurry, which didn't happen often. Well, one day at Upware we'd been planning to shut down round about lunch time, 'cos the water had been shifting nicely, and we'd turned the engine over about eight o'clock that morning. I'd just fired up, and got a real good head of steam going, so I though to myself 'Well, now I can have a quick fag and sit down and watch the world go by for a minute or two.'

Well, my old stoker had always dinned it into me never to pass my water gauge without checking it. So I did that without thinking. That was pretty low. So I opened the water valve and stood and waited. Nothing happened. Blimey! We're in trouble.

I opened the engine room door and yelled for the engine driver, Charlie, and he come tumbling down the stairs. I said "Look, mate – I'm just stoked up, two furnaces full of coal, and I haven't got any water. What the hell am I going to do?" I must admit I didn't feel all that good, all at once. "Nip you up and check the water pump" I told him, "something's wrong up there." Away he goes, and comes back and tells me that one of the connectors is broken, and if we didn't get the fires out the engine would likely explode, and us with her. Well, you can imagine how that made me feel. We couldn't let the steam valve off by sitting on it, because we didn't have enough head of steam up at that point.

So Charlie grabbed the long hoe, a bloomin' great thing all of twelve foot long, and I had to use that to rake all the live coal from the two furnaces. I should think that was one of the warmest jobs I've ever had to do. That's the God's own truth, I burned the soles of my shoes through. I never understood until then why they made the floors of boiler houses with cobbles - it was so that if there was hot ash lying around, you could rake it into the gaps between the stones and still hop about on top without danger. But in this case we were talking about more than just ash - Charlie was raking the live coals out into the yard, and then he went up and stopped the engine. But when the gaffer came round to see what had happened, he swore at the pair of us, he said if them fusible plugs had melted, all that water and high pressure steam, to say nothing of red-hot coals, would have spewed out over us. I reckon today I'd just say 'Right, that's it, I'm off,' and run for it, but in them days I was just young. And it would have been cowardice, wouldn't it, we had to stay there and get those fires out.

I haven't told you how we got our coal supply. It was kept in what was called the Coal Yard, a great heap of huge blocks of coal, and do you know no matter how expensive coal was for us to buy for the house, we never thought of taking any of that for our own use. We used to keep a pig too, in the coal yard, and chickens. And I don't know why, but that lovely yellow flower called Evening Primrose, that used to flourish in there. But anyhow, I'm digressing again. Coal came to the engine by barge. It was unloaded by barrows, damn great old things six or eight foot wide. Carry three quarters of a ton, they would, no kidding. Two men came up river with the lighter, and drew up in front of the engine where a bit of the river bank had been turned into a kind of dock, to save it being worn away, do you see. These men were called nippers, and they'd push them barrows of coal up to the weigh bridge on planks and trestles. They wore an iron climber thing on their boots, so they didn't fall off. Sometimes you took on 200 tons of coal to replenish the engine. Because the problem was, when there was a flood and water was high, that was just when you needed lots of coal and just when it was most dangerous to try to get it delivered. So we loaded up the yard in summer, mostly.

I'll tell you about another thing we had to do during the summer, and I don't know of a worse one unless that's being the chaff-minder on a threshing tackle. But don't get me off on that subject, else we shall be here all night. Between the two boilers there's a bit of wall, the flue wall, only put up with sand and water, so you could knock it out with a hammer. And then you are confronted with a great heap of grey powder. Soot that's been burned again and again isn't black, it's grey. Almost white. So you get on your hands and knees and in you crawl, until you can see right up that big chimney, like looking up a tube eight foot high. And even in daylight, you can actually see some of the stars, I suppose that's because you're in blackness and all light's cut off. Any rate, you have to go in head first, you can't turn round, no room to do that, and you have a wooden scraper to pull the stuff out, and it was like a lot of face powder. You got two bob extra and a bar of carbolic soap when you'd done that job, so as you could go straight out and wash in the river before you dared go anywhere and put dust all over the shop.

Now looking at me, you can see I'm quite a decent sized chap, I always had broad shoulders though I was slim when I was young, and I was quite strong. And at Upware, and then at Stretham, I had to get into that little hole at the bottom of the boiler, and once they showed me how, it was easy, you raise your arms above your head and clasp your hands, and that lessens your shoulder width by about six inches and so you can wriggle in. You're inside that flue, that's wet, that's cold, that's what you might call a humbugging job if ever there was one. We had a little lamp. Like the one Aladdin has in the pantomime, and that used to smoke and stink, and you had to chip off all the limescale but not hit too hard else you'd go clean through. And you're only wearing your shirt, and them rivets don't half dig in, I can tell you. That's a job as requires what you might call fortitude, and at Upware Bill would be in one flue and I'd be in the other, and there would be the occasional Bang! as one of us dropped his scraper, and then some fine old language, so I'm glad the gaffer wasn't around to hear that!

I'll tell you a funny story of what happened at Reach. A rich farmer was about to pay his men their weekly wage, and he had a lot of money with him. In a kind of a bag which zipped across. And in the barn that day were three or four men, and they were loading corn or something. Anyway, there were lots of bags of corn in the barn, and he laid this bag down while he reprimanded the foreman for something or other, and one of the workmen whipped this bag up and shoved it into a sack which contained wheat. Now, the foreman, having been reprimanded, then began to shout at the men right left and centre, and hustled them and bustled them about so that this particular sack with the money was huddled hither and thither and completely lost. The farmer then went to look for his bag and the men said No, you didn't have it when you came in, you must have thought so, but you didn't. So he went out in high dudgeon. Now this money was judged as being lost. I don't need to enlarge on this side of the story. And, er, then came the problem, how were they going to get this money. So anyway, they all decided that they would pinch the whole lot, they'd take all the sacks that were there. Which, surprisingly enough, they did. They put bags around the horses necks, they tied bags around the iron-shod wheels of the tumble carts and in the dead of night they loaded up the carts with these ten sacks of wheat and by going right across in front of these particular four men's houses they stole all this corn and only those four men really knew anything about it.

So when I say to you that these people of the fens were pretty lawless, it'd be absolutely true, because they were, and they were very strong characters. Hereward fought William the Conqueror and was what I think they now call a guerrilla fighter in the Isle of Ely, then there was Cromwell who overthrew another King. Then last but very much not least there were the Ely and Littleport Riots, people who knew, - at least we assume they knew – the terrible consequences. Most of them were transported for life to Australia. But I think eleven of them were hanged and there's a tablet on the back of St. Mary's church in Ely which records these people's names. Nowadays, of course, people get a bit of a kick out of saying "Yes, of course, so-and-so, well he was my great great grandfather, or a relation of my father, or something like that. Times have changed, haven't they, and we rather think it's fun to be a relative of someone who's a bit lawless. But nonetheless, these fens were the hide-out of the outlaw, the reprobate, the highwayman and lots of unpleasant characters. I think a lot of this has brushed off on the generations that lived here in the time of my grandfather. Now he could remember someone who was transported, and he served his time in Australia and he came back for the express purpose of "getting" the local big man, you know, the squire, and he came to my grandfather's house and they sat and talked well into the night and he told my grandfather he was a butcher, which of course as you realise in the Australia of those days was another form of highwayman or outlaw, and anyway, my grandfather sort of talked him out of this terrible vengeance that he had planned, and my grandfather told me this with great relief. He never would tell me the man's name, though.

* * * *

It is almost time to meet my mother, who was quite a scribbler. Before we hear what life was like for her, in many ways similar to things I have described in my own childhood, I have to put forward one more thought, that my father was an opportunist. There is no doubt that he was good looking, and from someone, perhaps Linda, he had inherited an ability to charm which lasted until he was a very old man. But although he would in later years snort with derision about 'juvenile delinquents' and boys from broken families, he had, I think, a very large chip on his shoulder from being brought up in what we would today call a dysfunctional family. As he grew into his late teens, he acquired a reputation as a trouble maker, and in his twenties, when he went into certain pubs in Ely everyone would very quietly move down the bar away from him, because – and he would boast of this – no-one knew if he would order a pint or knock someone down first. He would come home drunk and sleep in the outhouse, and Linda would call him a stupid fool. But there were any number of girls around in the village to succumb to his smile and his silver tongue, and he had a steady job as an engine stoker; life must have seemed good.

Father aged 28

Then, all at once, he was almost thirty, and not married. He'd been courting a Romany girl when he was working with steam ploughs, and told me once that her father, the head of the clan, had offered him his own vardo [gipsy wagon] and eventual head-ship if he married her, but somehow that came to nothing. As did his liaisons, however innocent, with girls from Stretham who by now were mostly married and raising children. Time to look around, assess what to do next. Which is when he saw my mother, a fairly plain little lass, quite dumpy, but in her favour she was the daughter of his boss at Stretham Engine, and so one day I think he stage-managed a meeting by going round to the back door when he knew full well Mr. Stevens was away, and turned the full battery of his courting skills on her. What I do know is that she loved him hopelessly and totally for the rest of her life. His own feelings suffered a sea-change after her early death but while they were together his nick-name for her was Chub, scarcely flattering, and he would say she was his little Suffolk Punch, short in the leg, big in the barrel and thick round the neck. When he went to concerts in church or chapel in which she was singing, he would nudge me and whisper 'There goes your mother!' Whatever his feelings for her, or his motives, she was much better educated than him, her parents were staunch members of the Methodist flock, and marrying her would do a great deal to get him back into what he used to refer to as 'the paths of righteousness'. I think he decided, just as his mother had made up her mind, that he would marry her and I also believe that she never questioned him as to why. When I study the wedding photo, all I can see in my father's expression is 'Look what I've managed to do' but perhaps I am being less than just.

My mother was, as I have said, nothing particular to look at. She was short, 4ft 10½ ins, which she maintained was due to being dropped on her head on a pile of dam-boards when she was small, but as I recollect it her mother, Grandma Stevens, was also tiny. She had a sweet smile but was really quite a timid person. Both her parents were fervent 'primitive' Methodists, and the doctrine they followed seems to have soaked into her really deeply. The only time she seems to have stood up against them was when my father made his intentions clear. Gran Stevens said in deep disgust "But he drinks!" and apparently mother turned on her and said that was no problem, and she was going to marry him whatever they thought. She then left the Methodist congregation for the Church of England, where she was duly married in 1936.

She was a great one for arguing with herself, and I think the only person I knew who could loose such an argument. She also had a fine disregard for instruction booklets, maintaining that she knew how to use whatever piece of machinery was in question, then becoming exasperated when it wouldn't work. She told me once of the occasion when the ammeter of the little Austin car she drove started charging backwards. She took the car to old Mr. Ellwood in the garage at Stretham, who was puzzled as to how she had managed to get the two terminals on the battery on the wrong way round, because one of them was large and one small. She confessed that she had hit them with a spanner until they fitted. That was typical of her.

She had her tragedies. It seems that she had promised she would look after the birth control situation, but there too she seems to have mis-read the instruction booklet, because she became pregnant on her honeymoon and seven months later gave birth to my elder sister who was hastily named Linda and who died that same day. Little or nothing was ever said about that, until many years later when I too miscarried of a first child though at a very early stage. On a subsequent visit to London my father drew me to one side and said confidentially that if my husband didn't 'come near me' for some time, that was to be expected. I then began to put two and two together and remember a few things. I think he blamed my mother not just for the pregnancy but the premature birth and the death of his daughter. It was 1941 before she persuaded him that the world was in such a state, perhaps there might not be much of a future and that they should try again, resulting in my birth in 1942. It does not show him in a particularly pleasant light.

Here is my mother's story.

LIVING AT THE HUNDRED FOOT ENGINE

The Hundred Foot Engine

My father was Engine Driver at Metheringham Fen Engine, in Lincolnshire, when I was conceived but they moved in June 1911 to The Hundred Foot Engine where he became Superintendent.

My first memory is of something I could not possibly have known, but it was related in such a way, and so often, that it became part of me. The slightly premature arrival of a girl child who might, or might not live. The mother, already into middle age and with two children, exhausted after a long labour. It was a home birth – what else should it be in 1911? Someone sent out to fetch the parson to the house, and then no-one could find a suitable vessel for water for the christening until one of the neighbours rushed in with a soup tureen. In which rather undignified way I became Gwendoline Stevens

A much clearer memory which creeps in here is of a day when I stood nervously by my mother's side, holding on to her apron. I was a scrawny child, and timid and the School Attendance Officers who had come to the house to see why I was still not in school one whole term after my 5th birthday seemed much bigger and more imposing than they could really have been. Mother was a gentle person, who would rarely snap at me, or even my brother at his most mischievous, although I have heard her sigh that if Edgar could find the dirtiest route home, he would always take it, but she swung round then and pointed through the kitchen window. 'Do you see that? And that?' She indicated the bare blue gault of the bank top, scythed by an easterly wind, the track at its base a droveway ridged high by cart wheels with ruts deep enough to hold a sack of potatoes, full of icy water. 'You expect me to send a child her size out along that? I'll see your neck as long as my arm before I let her anywhere near your precious school – and you can tell them that!' I don't remember their reaction, but it is certain that I didn't start school until the summer term when the ways were a little less foul.

In a sense my father was coming back home. For 200 years there have been Stevens in the Fens, all of them involved in farming or drainage work. His own grandfather, James Stevens, had run The Hundred Foot engine in his day. James' father came from Oxlode, a younger son of his was engine driver at Ten Mile Bank in the 1860's, William was blacksmith at The Hundred Foot until about 1876 and kept The Five Alls as well, being unable to subsist on a blacksmith's meagre salary. He then took over the smithy at Pymoor and became Post Master but in 1880 he, too, became an engine driver at the Swaffham and Bottisham engine, confusingly situated at Upware.

Swaffham Engine was one of the finest and largest erected in the fens, as well as being one of the last to be built. The advent of the centrifugal pump had made scoop wheels redundant, but Swaffham was 80 nominal horse power and cost, in 1850, almost £90,000. Strange, therefore, that it is best remembered for its one breakdown.

The flood of 1897 was severe, and by February 7th the water in the River Cam was topping over the banks. The Engine was running day and night with a full load and both boilers working at full pressure. On February 10th there was a loud 'Crack' and the sound of breaking machinery – the crankshaft, which connected the base of the con-rod to the flywheel, had snapped leaving the 20-foot long con-rod to plunge wildly around, banging against the wall of the engine house. The Engine would have slowed down of its accord as the eccentric ceased to drive the valves, but steam had to be shut off quickly to prevent damage. Now the main steam valve was in the boiler house, and William had to make his way round the racing machinery, shut off the steam and then get back into the Engine Room to stop the Engine itself. He was an imperturbable man, and one or some courage. In spite of his 64 years he reacted quickly, because once the great beam had lifted again the fine, intricate ball-bearing system would have shattered and the whole construction could have collapsed in ruins. Dodging the swinging con-rod he reached the steam inlet control, turned it off and ordered the fires to be pulled out. He then returned to the Engine House, took the starting handle down from the wall where it hung, and tried to engage it, but with the Engine still running, he must just have dropped it in, hoping it would find its own position. He then had to use that handle to work the valves in the opposite direction, rather like the way a jet plane stops by going into reverse thrust. In other words, he had to let steam in at the bottom as the piston was coming down. Not an easy job, but William was an experienced man, and his prompt action saved the Engine to serve the District for another 40 years.

When my father came to The Hundred Foot in 1911, where I was born that September, the beam engine was still in its place and working but the problem of peat shrinkage was already making itself felt and the scoop wheel was finding it more and more difficult to lift the water sufficiently high to get it into the river. So in 1914 a big marine diesel engine was installed coupled to a centrifugal pump which could handle much bigger lifts. It was a time of great upheaval. There were workmen to stay while they did the job first of all of breaking up the dismantled beam engine and then installing the new one. My brother was put in the small bedroom where I used to have my cot and I went into Norfolk to stay with my aunt who at the time had no children of her own, being younger than mother.

Aunt Lil had a severe cast in one eye and perhaps I have superimposed memories of her from later times, because at two years old I couldn't have noticed much, but it was always difficult working out whether she was looking at you or somewhere else in the room. She had a strong Norfolk accent which made it all the harder to understand her, and if I came home - as my mother maintained - spoilt past bearing it was probably because Aunt Lil let me do more or less what I wanted, being unable to communicate with this strange, silent little creature who had been foisted on her. When I was staying with her a few years later, I asked timidly where the broom was kept as she had asked me to sweep the kitchen floor for her. "That hang hind of the shed door," she snapped at me. "Least, dew that don't do that did!" which made perfect sense to her if not much to me.

I was fascinated by the big diesel engine. It seemed to have two mouths in its middle which clacked open and shut. I suppose they were valves of some kind. My father would often let me into the engine to watch him go round and adjust the drip feeds and oil certain areas. He had to clean out the filters from time to time in the big concrete cooling tank behind the engine and often there were small fish caught in it, which he would throw back into the big drain. On one memorable day something different wriggled out - a lamprey, a sucker fish, the sort that King John ate too many of and died.

Father also told me as he worked various tales about local people, engineers he'd known. Talking to himself as much as me, I suppose, because the sound of the big engine was monotonous and the atmosphere stuffy, and probably keeping awake was something of a job. Especially during times of high water when he would probably run the engine for a day and two nights, having only a brief break for sleep while his stoker took over. Sometimes he made me laugh. One of his workmen had been digging a new drain in the depths of the fen and came racing across to the Engine halfway through the day. Apparently he was sitting down on the edge of his new excavation, having his dockey of bread and onion, when something sneezed behind him. He leapt up and turned round, but there was nothing in sight for several flat miles. He told my father he reckoned it was a Hobyar. I think father realised that it was only one of his colleagues hiding down in the green wheat, but certainly there were some very strange things that went on in the fen and I, for one, have always kept an ear tuned, in case I hear a Hobyar sneeze.

There were more terrifying stories than that. Father told me never, never to step across the spinning shaft which worked the centrifugal pump in the diesel engine, because he'd seen a man do that and, as he stooped over, his coat caught in it. Before he could do anything, he was whipped round the shaft, and there he lay with his neck broken.

GOING TO SCHOOL IN PYMOOR

I have related earlier how I was kept back from school until the summer term. I had at least three miles of black fen roads to cover to get there, as the school was half a mile from the village of Pymoor. It had been built at one end of a grass field. The playground was a mixture of gravel and dust in summer, gravel and mud in winter. The school had two rooms. The larger of them was for the 8 to 14-year olds, and opening from that was the room for the Infants. There was one small basin to wash your hands, and the water for that came from the ditch which ran down the side of the school field. We drank that same water at lunch time – could have been worse as it was no more than rainwater, no sewage or land chemicals in it. During the last year of the Great War we had cups of cocoa supplied in the winter term,. And those parents who had the money paid 2d a day. It was a somewhat harsh-tasting brew and I think we took saccharine tablets with us to sweeten it.

For lunch we took sandwiches, as we came from far and wide and going home for lunch would have been impossible. We often started to eat them on the way to school which meant that we were hungry for the rest of the day. Sometimes we would go what we called 'the long way round' to get home which meant we could go along a made-up road heavily clotted with lumps of mud from the farm carts. Occasional repairs were made by dumping great pieces of flint in the more obvious holes, and woe betide any child who fell on one of them. They were less than sympathetic to bare knees. Going round by the road meant passing one or two farms and one of them had an early form of carrot washing machine. If he saw us coming, he'd give a grin and throw half a dozen carrots across the road, which we gladly gnawed on.

The fens may look bleak and regimented, but the river banks themselves were, in the days of my childhood, a treasury of wild flowers. In early Spring sheets of coltsfoot would appear, rather marvellous to me because they flowered before their leaves came up. Dandelions followed them and we played the traditional game of 'Sniff one and you'll wet the bed' which, I believe, refers to the dandelion as a diuretic though we knew nothing of such matters. When the daisies appeared, if you could put your foot on three at once, then it was Spring. Tall pink mallows gave us their hard little green fruits to nibble. We called them mallow cheeses. There were masses of cow parsley. Purple thistles came later, hard on our bare legs but the bees and butterflies loved them. The hedges were frothed with may blossom, as we called the hawthorn, and wild roses. One of my favourite games was to get an empty matchbox and try to catch bumble bees from the thistles, some of which were as tall as me. I was never stung, though I don't know why.

Wandering along the river bank was something I loved to do. It wasn't exactly a safe place for a child, but in those days we accepted that if we were told not to do something there was a good reason and we didn't, on the whole, try it. My brother was the exception to that rule, but more of him later on. The river was tidal and at high tide the water stretched across from one barrier bank to the other, obliterating the washland between. Often I have watched my father 'gleaving' for dabs on a Spring evening when the salt tide came up. I think they were a kind of flat-fish that lived in the silts of The Wash. His gleave was made by the local blacksmith, and was mostly used for catching eels. It consisted of a fan of about six flat blades so made that they had a certain amount of flexibility, fixed to the end of a long pole. The art was not to try to spear the fish, but to trap them between the blades. Fried in butter they were a delicious treat. Other rubbish, driftwood and rushes, also came up on the tide and round about October was collected eagerly by us children ready for Guy Fawkes Night when we had a big bonfire, though not many fireworks.

We walked along the bank to the farm half a mile away where we could buy a can of separated milk for a penny. This was used for puddings, and my mother would put shredded suet in it to replace the fat content. But we didn't use this milk in our tea, because father kept a goat. This animal was a source of amazement to me. She had more mischief in her than most. One evening, father, mother and I went out for a walk. The goat was staked out on the bank with a strong chain, but when we strolled home she met us quite a way up the bank, dragging her tether behind her. In her goatish way she was laughing, lifting her top lip and bleating at us. My father declared that she had been 'up to something' and she had. She'd made her way into the vegetable garden and devoured a whole row of two inch high pea plants. This must have been pure mischief, because she was always well fed with chopped mangolds and other things as well as what she could graze from her stake.

On one occasion she was really frightened. The boilers at the Engine were high pressure and one day one of them blew its safety valve with a terrific roar. The goat pulled out her stake and took off down the field behind the Engine. We didn't see her for a week, until someone enquired from a couple of miles away if we'd lost a goat, because they'd found one.

The farm from which we fetched the milk also supplied us with butter, and sometimes after a cow had calved we had a large jug of 'beesnins' as we called the first milk drawn off after the birth. I suppose we were robbing the calf of its nourishment, but the farmer's wife told me once that a good cow would produce too much for a calf to start with, and it would only go to waste. This rich creamy substance was mixed with ordinary milk and sugar, and some raisins if we had any, sprinkled with nutmeg and baked in the oven as a delicious pudding..

When I became older I was allowed to fish in the river, if I was careful. I didn't have a proper fishing rod, which was for my older brother of course. But a stout piece of willow had sufficient flexibility, with a long piece of fine string tied to the end and a cruel-looking black eel hook. If we were lucky we would find lost floats and other bits of tackle after the tide had gone down. I know I was thrilled to accumulate enough pocket money to buy a proper float, it was green below and red above and 'bobbed' beautifully. I caught a good many eels which mother would skin and clean, cut into lengths and stew. They were served with parsley sauce and a dash of vinegar.

Sometimes as we stood on the edge of the actual river course, we would hear a low roaring noise away down towards Denver. Then lines would be hastily pulled out, rods snatched up and we would beat a retreat to the bank top because the tidal bore was approaching. Steadily the noise would increase, the water would swell until along came a great rounded wave as much as three feet above the normal level of water, which didn't break, just hissed along the sides of the river among the rushes. Often it almost reached Earith before it dropped away.

Many things were brought up the river in boats, the big horses steadily pulling into their collars and plodding along the tow path. Fish for sale, cockles, winkles and mussels from the coast, and of course coal for the Engine from Kings Lynn. I was always kept indoors when there was a coal delivery, 'just in case' as my mother would say, but I think it was probably because of the somewhat racy language of the lightermen. The coal yard where the coal was stored was a big brick and slate building, and one of the windows had broken panes through which pigeons used to fly and nest in the eaves. One evening my father decided pigeon pie was on the menu, so armed with a long stick he went on a crusade, knocking down the birds. I was supposed to put them in a basket, but being soft-hearted I would let out through the Engine Room door any that seemed still able to fly. Father never could understand why he had so few birds. In fact it was one of the very few times that I heard him use what was for him strong language. 'That caps my arse why I didn't get more birds,' he said, as he stumped back into the house.

THE FIVE ALLS

– a public house near where I lived.:

- The Queen Rules All
- The Lawyer Pleads for All
- The Doctor Cures All
- The Parson prays for All
- The Farmer pays for All

I was brought up on strictly teetotal stock and to this day am physically unable to drink anything alcoholic without becoming ill. But the elderly couple at the Five Alls were friendly with my parents and the place itself used to fascinate me. Sometimes the landlady would let me clean out the taproom and scatter fresh sharp sand on the floor of yellow bricks. I was allowed to go down into the cellars, one opening out of the other, and see the huge beer barrels in the wooden racks. The pub was the only place men could meet, apart from the chapel which wasn't quite the same atmosphere! Drunkenness wasn't frequent, the beer was pretty thin stuff I think, but what happened at Christmas or Bank Holidays was a different matter. One old fellow named Jim would have something like fourteen pints on Christmas morning. He lived about half a mile away, up towards the big railway bridge and as I have said often, the top of the bank was a well-trodden footpath. A couple of less inebriated men would propel Jim up to the top of the bank, where he could walk in a more or less straight line until he reached the path leading down to his cottage. Getting down this was too much for him, and he used to lie down and roll to the bottom, at which point one of his children would run out and call to his wife 'Mother, the daft old fool's home again."

We had a duty that took us along the bank top daily, as far as the railway bridge. Only two families had a daily paper, ours being one of them, but it wasn't delivered by a newsboy. It came by train from Ely. As the train slowed up for the bridge approach the guard would take aim and fling the two wrapped and rolled newspapers on to the bank. Sometimes they fell short so then, greatly daring, we would run out to grab them from the rail track itself.

The muddy track at the bottom of the bank was used only for heavy traffic, such as the steam engine and threshing tackle. On one occasion the engine slipped sideways on an exposed patch of gault clay and no matter what they tried, they couldn't get her upright again. Being a nosey little parker, I was hanging around watching this and heard one of the men say 'Tha's a right bugger,' so for a good many years I thought that was the correct title for a traction engine in a ditch. Fortunately I didn't ask my mother – I don't know what she would have said, but I think she would have curbed my liberty considerably. Various tradesmen brought carts along to the yard of The Five Alls, and mother and I usually went down in case there was some knick-knack we fancied. Then there was the occasion when the butcher's cart had an accident, right outside our house. He came weekly from the village of Littleport in a two-wheel trap, in the back mysterious hunks of meat which would be cut down to order. The only gesture towards hygiene was a jug of vinegar in which the knives were plunged after each session of carving. But they had to be taken out and dried on an old cloth as they were not stainless, so whether that had any effect I don't know. One evening he came up towards our house and just as he arrived, the belly-band which passes under the horse's stomach to keep the cart from tipping suddenly gave way. Up flew the shafts and all the meat tumbled into the fen mud. Mr Palmer and my mother made no fuss, fetched it into our house where it was washed and pushed back on to the cart. The belly-band was mended with a length of string and off he went along the bank. I suppose you could say it all went to thicken the gravy!

BIRTHS, DEATHS AND ACCIDENTS

Perhaps it was because we lived in the 'big house' that it was to us people came for first aid. There was, of course, no National Health Service and visits to the doctor cost money, which was in short supply. If a man could feed and clothe his family from his wages, he was doing well. Besides, the journey into the fen would put off most doctors. Dire emergencies were another thing. I owe my life to one doctor who, when I contracted acute pneumonia at the age of 15, came out daily to our house. I seemed fated to suffer more than the average child. I had pneumonia twice and whooping cough three times which must have daunted even my mother's spirits.

Sometimes the treatment was pretty primitive. We used to ride around in a small cart called a Governess Cart with a door in the back. I cannot remember how old I was, but I managed to have my finger in the way when that little door was slammed shut. To my parents' horror half of the top joint of my finger was almost completely amputated, held on only by a flap of skin. Father whipped up the donkey and we made it to the doctor's, where all he could do was to dip the raw end of my finger in iodine. At that point I fainted, but he stuck the detached joint back on top of the open wound, and bound it tight. I was lucky that it was the very finger tip, where the nerves and capillaries are few and far between, but I still don't know who was more surprised, me, my parents or the doctor, when my finger actually healed up and I regained almost all the sensation although it was crooked at the tip from that day on.

On one occasion I came close to losing my father. He had been trimming some dam boards with an adze. It glanced off a knot in the wood and hit his shin with sufficient force to sever a vein. The nearest doctor was seven miles away, in Ely, the nearest phone three miles away at the village Post Office. So Ely it had to be. My mother wadded the leg with several layers of old cloth, as she couldn't stop the bleeding. Then she managed to get father on to his bicycle, and with him using his other leg to propel himself and her helping to keep him upright, they made it to a farm where the farmer had a car. So father got to Ely and the wound was stitched. Had it been an artery, I imagine he would have bled to death on the way.

There were funnier moments, too. Mrs Leaford who kept the Five Alls was doing her weekly wash one Monday. Washing was done by hand in a large tin bath or in a wooden wash-keeler. The whites went into the copper, where a good fire was needed under it to keep them boiling. On that particular day the fire wouldn't draw, so she took a cartridge from her husband's pouch, tore off the end and threw the gunpowder onto the fire under the copper. There was an almighty bang, and far from clearing the chimney, the door of the furnace was blown off into her face. When mother went hurrying round to see what the noise was about, there was Mrs Leaford with a face as black as the end man in a minstrel show, her front hair and her eyebrows completely singed off.

THE LITTLE CHAPEL

This held at the most seventy people but was the centre of activity for most of the women and some of the men too. It was plainly built, rectangular, with a tiny porch at the front. The windows had a surround of coloured glass, there was a small organ which had to be pumped by foot pedals and of course the louder you wanted to play, the faster you had to pedal. My mother was usually the organist, both parents played a part in the Morning Service and there was Sunday School at 2.30 p.m. with a final Evening Prayer at half past six. So in our house Sunday was scarcely a day of rest. Before we all left for the morning service the big black coal range would be stoked up and the damper pulled out. Mother would put the joint in the oven and mix the Yorkshire pudding. As soon as the preacher at morning service got up to speak, I would wriggle out of chapel, hurry along home, boost up the fire and put the pudding into the oven, lay the potatoes round the joint and set the table so that by the time mother and father had heard the sermon, sung a final hymn and done the rounds of meeting people, dinner would just about be cooked.

The non-conformist Minister from Ely who had our chapel under his care could only come over to us once each quarter, and the rest of the services were conducted by a dedicated band of Local Preachers who often cycled as much as ten miles each way to preach. On one occasion my own father cycled nineteen miles each way, but I think that distance was unusual. They may not have been men of great learning, but they were totally sincere in their religious beliefs. They would be invited to tea by one of the better-off members of the tiny congregations they ministered to. We often 'had the preacher to tea' which was quite a carry on, involving that rarity, a tin of red salmon, if at all possible, or something I still enjoy, a pig's head brawn, lovely served with vinegar and some brown bread and butter. There would be a blancmange too, and mother would bake a heavy fruit cake. One regular visitor to us used to bring mother watercress when he visited, but because she didn't know where he picked it. Watercress will grow wherever there is moving water, but is rather careless as to whether that water is clean or contaminated. She would get one of us children to go out into the fen to find some in clean water and his offering would in due course be fed to the chickens. I remember being very proud indeed one Sunday to be able to offer a saucer of mustard and cress which I had grown on an old piece of flannel on the windowsill. Simple pleasures, and I wonder if today's children get as much from all their complex toys.

That same local preacher also smoked a pipe and one Sunday he put it in his pocket, still warm, as he approached the Chapel. During the sermon, which was a traditional rant about hell-fire and judgement, we were amazed to see wisps of smoke rising from the pulpit. He had not knocked out all the dottle from his pipe which was smouldering in his pocket. Nothing daunted, when he realised he stepped down from the pulpit, went out, dealt with the problem and came back to finish what he had to tell us. We children were most impressed.

The Sunday School Anniversary was held on the third Sunday in June. The day before, planks and trestles would be fetched from the barn of the Five Alls where, by some strange tradition they were kept.. A high platform was built at the front of the chapel, and we girls would know that a night of torment was ahead of us as our long hair would be bound up in 'curling rags' after our bath, so as to grace the occasion. But how proud we were in our best dresses, with curls to our waists, to climb up the step ladder on to the platform and sit behind the decorated guard rail. Some would recite, others would sing special hymns learned for the occasion, and at the end we would all take part in a presentation that involved holding a square of card with a letter on it, and turning the card over so that some word or other or a short bible text would be revealed.

TREATS

Armistice Day, 1918. The day I was smacked, and hard, by my big sister. I scarcely knew her. She was 12 years older than me, and had been in one of the women's services for the duration of the Great War. Where she learned to smoke! I was 7 years old, and this strange grown-up woman, as I saw her, came to live with us. She couldn't smoke in the house, so she went down by the river. I followed her, being like most children a curious little grub of a child, and saw what she was doing. So I ran to my mother, and snitched to her. My sister chased me into the boiler house of the engine and gave me a good hiding, Armistice Day or no. Looking back, I can see that the War, for her, was liberation and I don't think my parents were all that surprised when she went off to Canada, where she married Dick Matthews and began the Canadian section of our family, my cousins Dick, Pat and Sheila and all their offspring. I'll be fair to my sister, though. Because it was a day of celebration, and because our family had survived without bereavement, once the smacking was over she said, "Now come and give me a hug, and let's try to be friends." Later that day my mother dressed up in some of my brother's pyjamas and I shall always remember her capering up and down the bank. My irrepressible brother had blackened his face too and was doing his own capering. I don't know why they were collecting, probably for the families of the bereaved, but he went round to one cottage and the sight of him caused the lady there to collapse in a faint. Her baby was born the next day and even when he was a grown man, my brother used to claim responsibility for the child, which brought disapproving looks from some of the more pious members of the Methodist congregation.

Then there was Little Downham Hospital Sunday, an annual event complete with a band, decorated floats and a festival tea for the children. Addenbrokes Hospital in Cambridge was at that time almost totally maintained by voluntary contributions so what was collected on that day was much appreciated. On the three evenings following, the Feast would be on the Green at Little Downham – swings and roundabouts, a rock stall where we could spend the few pennies our parents managed to give us. There were swing-boats too, and the boys would buy tin whistles which they would blow as they swung backwards and forwards, making a terrible noise. There was a big fair once a year at Ely, held on the market place, but as I was by then at the High School, even if my father was prepared to cycle in to meet me, it meant going to the Fair in my school uniform which we were strictly forbidden to do. So I had to be content with the lesser joys of Hospital Sunday and the Feast.

There were two more big days in the life of the chapel. One was Camp Meeting Sunday and I think we all prayed most heartily for a fine day. Services were not held indoors on that day, but we gathered on the river bank and listened to the preachers. The little pedal organ was brought out so that we could sing hymns, and instead of the pulpit those who were chosen to preach would do so from a farmer's cart. In the evening there was community singing, mostly hymns but none the less entertaining for that.

Harvest Festival was the other big occasion. We decorated our chapel with the best we could offer, fruit, vegetables, sheaves of corn and - joy of joys - a large bunch of black grapes from a local farmer who had what we would now call a conservatory with a grape vine in it. They hung at the focal point, over the centre of the pulpit. No-one seemed to connect them with wine and the demon alcohol, but more with Christ's saying 'I am the true Vine and ye are the branches'. The chapel had a large tortoise stove to heat it in really cold days and although it was not lit for Harvest Festival, there was some competition to grow an extra large marrow to decorate it. The Harvest hymns were sung at the two Sunday services, and on Monday there was another, shorter service which we children all attended with a few extra pennies in our pockets which we'd earned by doing little jobs around the house or the yard, because we knew that after the service would come the Harvest Tea and the sale of produce. We had no schoolroom attached to our chapel, so boards were laid across the pews to make a kind of raised platform and on that tables were erected. Best family lace and precious tea-services were brought out, carried usually in the family clothes basket. Woe betide any child who managed to break the handle off a cup! Extra thin bread and butter and two kinds of cake, both home made and "shop". With the perversity of children, we chose the junk food, the shop cake, every time.

Then came The Sale! The tables were cleared except for three which were pulled together to make a long counter where the produce from the harvest service was laid out, and a local man, usually one with a good gift for chat, was persuaded to take on the role of auctioneer. He could have sold coals to Newcastle, I do believe. Often we'd buy back apples from our own orchard, and there was the usual attempt to make Softy, the boy who was not quite right in his head as we used to say in those days, buy a huge bunch of very woody beetroot for his mother at a special price. Money raised went to help support the chapel funds. Sometimes one of the mothers would have saved enough butter and sugar to make some toffee and she would pass that down the lines of eager, fidgeting children. The young fellows congregated at the back, trying to outbid each other or buy something for their 'intended'. If there were any pastries or cakes left from the Tea, they too would be sold. One auctioneer, little knowing that young Fred had called in at the Five Alls on his way for a couple of pints, said "Come you on, Fred, gimme a price for these tarts, your mouth's just the right size for one of they." Fred muttered darkly to those around him that he'd make someone's mouth a different shape if he didn't hold his noise. Fortunately for all of us he was quietly eased out of the crowd by a couple of his mates before any damage could be done.

MY BROTHER

Edgar has appeared briefly throughout my narrative, but he really deserves a section to himself. I think I worshipped him. As I have said, my elder sister was a stranger and soon left home again anyway. But Edgar was a lovable scamp. He would give me rides on the handlebars of his old bike, but was likely to swoop up the side of a potato clamp and down again, or go full pelt through a huge puddle, so I ended up splashed and dirty or fell off and grazed my knees. Only the fact that the droveways were of soft peat soil saved me, I am sure, from more serious injury..

Like all local lads, he used to collect birds eggs, and he had set his heart on a rook's egg from the Holt, the little clump of trees near the Railway Bridge. On the way home from school one April evening he climbed up a tree while we little ones looked on in amazement at his daring. He found some eggs but was too scared to put one in his pocket so he popped it into his mouth. Halfway down the tree, he lost his footing and slid, bumped and rolled the rest of the way down. The egg broke in his mouth, and to his disgust it was addled, which in later years he would say quite took away his taste for birds-nesting.

When he was told to clean his bike, he simply attached it to a rope and threw it into the river, but the end of the rope jerked out of his hands, and if it hadn't landed in a bed of reeds where he could just reach it, that would have been that.

Mince pies were home-made in those days and the lids could be prised up. So that is exactly what he did, scooping out the mincemeat and replacing the lids which -dreadful as it seems – he stuck back down with a bit of spit! The ladies from the Bright Hour who were visiting my mother were not impressed. Thinking of those afternoon gatherings, I remember one visitor who always said she would be able to tell when goat's milk was in the tea, as she would be sick, but when she came to our house she asked mother for a second cup, saying it was the best she'd ever tasted.

Edgar once stayed with our relations in Norfolk. They had a shop, and he went down into the cellar and turned the tap on the vinegar barrel so that sloshed all over the floor. Seeing that no drastic punishment resulted, he did the same with the molasses barrel, which I think did lead to a good hiding, and rightly so because molasses must have been very difficult to clear up. Be that as it may, he didn't go to stay with them again.

During one very frosty spell when the washes were transformed into a giant skating rink, he persuaded my mother to bake some small scones and buns. He wrapped these in a cloth and pedalled swiftly to the bridge where, according to one old man who told me this, he 'hollered out 'Hot Cakes, tuppence a go'' and sold the lot.

Even being in chapel couldn't damp down his naughtiness. One of the Bible readings was about how the whale 'spewed up Jonah' at which Edgar stood up and pretended to be sick, very loudly.

And during one Anniversary the special hymn we had learned finished with a rousing chorus 'When we get to heaven we shall wear a crown'. By then Edgar's voice was starting to break, and in his new *basso profundo* he added, 'Upside down'. It wasn't funny at the time.

* * * *

Before my mother continues her memories, it is time to meet her brother from a different point of view as my Uncle Edgar, together with my renowned Auntie Bea and their two children, my cousins Grahame and Felicity. Grahame was just that much older than me to be of no interest, treating me rather loftily. He had his own 'gang' and Uncle Edgar had put up a little shed in their back garden as gang HQ, where no doubt they conducted all the strange rituals that teenagers are fond of. Gwen Beasley, Denis Cockerton, Chris Lythel, I remember some of their names. They were allowed to boil a kettle on old oil stove in the hut, I believe, and make drinks, which seemed a real adventure to me.

Uncle Edgar was mild-mannered, silver-haired, rotund but quick on his feet and a champion bowls player with many trophies to his name. I had learned to keep on the right side of Auntie Bea, who had a rather elevated sense of her own importance and an exaggerated drawly voice. But Uncle never bothered. In fact it was suggested that a good title for his memoirs might have been 'Happy Daze'. Until he retired he had owned the garage on the Cambridge Road, which he ran in a similarly casual fashion, often not opening until 10.00 a.m. and then working well into the evening. On a winter's afternoon when we were bored or feeling the cold, we'd find him sitting by the tortoise stove quietly mending someone's radio or fixing a puncture on a bicycle tyre. Often, I believe, for no charge. He was that kind of man. We would sit and watch as his deft fingers sorted a new valve or a length of wire from what looked like tumbled chaos on the bench, humming a little tune to himself. If friends of his dropped in, he'd say 'Off with you now. Uncle's got things to do'.

Each year he built an enormous bonfire for Guy Fawkes Night, saving the prunings from the orchard as a foundation. While he ran the garage he had waste oil to slosh around it so that it burned high and fierce. Then he would grab a pitchfork and caper around moving branches to and fro, causing showers of sparks while local children who had plotted and planned to be invited to the Bonfire Party would scatter and shriek with glee, and Auntie Bea, coming from the house with a tray of chocolate cake and ginger parkin, would say in despair 'Edgar dear, you'll set the house on fire!' But he never did.

One day in 1962, during the summer when I was home from College, my cousin Felicity and I had been playing tennis on the village court – well, more like knocking a ball to and fro, as our skills and the texture of the rough grass didn't make for much skilled play. It came on to rain and we adjourned to her house. Uncle Edgar was having a few moments rest in their front room. He'd been out seeing to the geese which were family pets, originally bought to keep down the grass in the orchard. They had individual names, though Auntie Bea said she couldn't tell one from another, and had originally been fetched in a pig-trolley towed behind the car, with a net fastened over the top so that they couldn't get out. Uncle used often to go and have long involved conversations with them and maintained that they understood every word he said.

Good smells were beginning to drift from the kitchen where Auntie Bea was doing some baking and, hoping the rain would carry on until tea time, we busied ourselves with a box of photographs and mementoes that had been brought from our late Grandmother's house. Eventually our giggling guesswork as to which photos were of which relatives woke Uncle, just as my cousin pulled out a Christmas card, on the front a ribbon bow of maroon and royal blue and the words No. 6 Armoured Car Company, Royal Air Force Kirkuk, Mesopotamia wrapped round the official badge. Inside was a simple greeting with the added words 'To my dear parents, much missed at this time of year, from Edgar'.

Uncle leant forward and twitched the card out of her hand. 'So she did keep it, after all' he said with a little smile. 'Yes, I was over there for several years.' He puckered up his face and sang a couple of lines of something:

But when 'e got to Basrah, 'e met a great big 'awk
Wot plucked orff all 'is fevers and sez 'Nah yer can bloomin' well walk`

"Tell, tell," we begged.

"All right. If you sit quietly." He thought for a minute or two. "Well, I left school," he said eventually. "I didn't want to work on the land. I'm no gardener, as you well know. But I had a gift for making mechanical things work. I built a crystal radio set once, but upset mother by using a giant sea-shell which was her pride and joy for the speaker, sawing the end off it to get the wires in. Anyway, they found me a job as a at Cass's garage in Ely. I was 14, nearly 15. It meant biking a long way each day to work, but everyone did that, and we didn't think too much of it. Now I don't remember exactly what I was up to, but mother told me I nearly caused an explosion before I'd been working there all that long. In fact if Mr. Cass hadn't come in when he did, he'd have been without a livelihood. So I was politely sent home to my parents, which makes me think my apprenticeship must have been a rather informal arrangement without indentures. Then someone mentioned to my parents that a good place for trainee engineers was the RAF at Cranwell. Which is how I ended up in Mesopotamia. Yes, I know it's Iraq now, but I still think of it by its old name. I was a Leading Aircraftman, then a Corporal.'

I asked him what the RAF was doing in Iraq at that time, between the two World Wars. He smiled. 'Looking after the oil-fields, my dear. We were there in a peace-keeping role. I had to maintain the armoured vehicles. Patrolling over those dirt roads certainly wore out the suspension. We used to wear nothing but shorts, boots and a sun helmet, it was that hot. There was a Vickers Vernon plane that had crashed, we used to let the little local boys sit in it and pretend to fly, and I think we charged them. The cheek of it. When we first got there we used to want to swim in the Tigris, but it's not called 'The Arrow' for nothing. Although the waters seem to move slowly, we were warned that the currents were treacherous, and then one day a Vickers Flying Boat tried to land on it, and we watched it pitch and toss while the crew tried to get a rope ashore. That cured us of wanting to go into it. But we made ourselves a kind of swimming pool in a feeder stream, which we dammed off with a great artificial sand dune. It was as warm as a bath, being in there. They were good days, for a fairly untutored Fen boy. More than my wildest dreams. There was a pomegranate tree in the garden of my billet in Hinandi. Like something in the Arabian Nights.

And once I was given the honour of driving the King to Baghdad – in fact my first driving licence was issued there, with Arabic writing on it.'

Had he finished? The good smells from the kitchen had intensified, and cups were being rattled around. 'Ah, Tea,' he said. 'Good. All that talking makes me thirsty. Oh, I'll tell you something else. You've heard of Lawrence of Arabia, no doubt seen the film too.'

We had, and I nodded. I knew something about Lawrence's latent homosexuality and wondered what was coming next.

'I met him. He'd joined the RAF under the name of Shaw. He shared our billet. He was a funny guy – wasn't happy to wash by way of jumping into our swimming pool a couple of times a day. No, he had to heat up great degshies of water on an old oil stove and wash himself that way. I used to like talking to him. He had some sensible ideas about how the Middle East should be governed. But our ways parted, and I was posted to Ur, the birth-place of Abraham. You'll probably find a postcard of the Ziggurat somewhere in that box. I remember sending one home. And we returned on HMT Nevassa. I was able to send my parents a card as we entered the Red Sea; 'Expect me in about four days from the time you get this.' I'd been away five years – left home as a lad and came back a man.'

He turned and looked out of the big side window, just as Auntie Bea came in with a tray. 'Has he been yarning again?' she enquired.

'Just telling them a bit about my time in Mesopotamia,' he said, reaching for a cup. 'But look, the rain's taken off. After tea you girls can finish that tennis game.' He glanced down at the Christmas card which he had been holding all the while, leant forward, replaced it in the box and firmly closed the lid.

* * * *

Now back to my mother's narrative.

TRANSPORT AND TRAVEL AT PYMOOR

How did we get around? Mostly we walked. Those who had a car used it, those who had access to a horse or donkey and cart went that way, some had bicycles and at the bottom of the list were the rest of us – so we walked. When my own turn came to have a bicycle I couldn't get the hang of the pedals at first, so I used to get on at the top of the bank and freewheel down it, falling off at the bottom into the soft fen dust. I know I got extremely dirty and my mother was puzzled as to why.

When I was 10 years old I won a scholarship to the High School in Ely. I had to go for an interview before being accepted, and it was a long ride for a small girl. The Headmaster of the school at Little Downham came to my rescue. "She'll never make it," he told my father. "Pop her bike on my running board and I'll get her there in style." I felt very grand, though I had to put my hand through the open car window and keep a firm hold of my bicycle all the way. It was a journey of seven miles each way for me, and I little realised that I would be doing it for the next seven years. In the summer it was pleasant enough and as the alternative would have been to walk, I suppose I was happy though I often arrived at school wet. But winter was a different matter. Being wet and cold too was taken seriously by the staff, but in Bedford House where the High School was then situated there were no radiators. Those of us who had suffered on our way to school stripped to our navy bloomers and liberty bodices and while our outer clothes were hung up to dry, we were placed in front of the dining room fire where we steamed gently until we were deemed fit to be clothed again.

Often the cold was too much to bear. The Fens are very open and an east wind can cut across them with almost knife-like precision. In fact my father used to call it a lazy wind, one that went through you rather than round you. I was used to having chafed thighs and chilblains, but one bitterly cold morning I remember coming down the hill from Little Downham and then suddenly nothing more until I came to my senses lying on the sofa in the Rectory. It seems I had fainted from the cold and fallen from my bicycle, to be rescued by the Rector's wife and brought into the warm. I didn't go to school that day – I was taken home by a farmer with a car, and I think my father walked out and rescued the bike from where I'd left it.

Sometimes my mother would go into Norfolk to see her mother and family, including Aunt Lil of the boss-eye. It was a complex journey. First the long walk to the little railway station on the Ely to March line, which even if we went up a drove or two was still three miles. The station was called Black Bank, and had one tiny waiting room doubling as a ticket office, with a few benches on the platform itself. There was an advertisement on a metal plate on the waiting room wall, and I was very proud to be able to spell out "Keatings kills fleas, flies, moths, bugs and beetles." My mother was not very enthusiastic. She herself kept a clean house, with no time for "little visitors" but one day while we were waiting for a late-running train she told me about their arrival at Metheringham Fen Engine, when they were a newly married couple. The bedrooms in the

Engineer's house had wallpaper on them, which was bulging and bubbled in places. Impatiently as any new owner thinking of redecorating, she pulled at one of these bubbles, thinking no doubt of how she'd soon have some fresh distemper on the walls. The paper split and out tumbled several colonies of bed-bugs. She and my father didn't wait to see what else might be hiding in the house. It was immediately closed for fumigation, and in the meantime the young couple actually slept and kept house on one of the landings of the beam engine, where it was warm and clean.

Our journey into Norfolk took us from Black Bank to Ely, where we had to change. The subway there always smelt of fish, though I don't think it was a station where a great deal of fish changed hands. It also curved, so I was allowed to run down to the bottom and peep round the upward curve to see if the train was in. It never occurred to me just to look across the line, or at least not until I was a lot older. The train we caught there went to Kings Lynn, where we changed yet again to what was in those days the Midland & Great Northern Line to South Lynn. Incredibly, we then changed finally to a train to Grimston. All that for a journey of some 30 miles which today would take half an hour in a car. Black Bank station has now completely disappeared, and the whole line to Grimston has been rooted up except for one embankment which runs across a piece of pastureland between Pott Row and Roydon and where, if you look carefully, the clinker showing through the grass will give away that it was once a railway bed.

Soon after that we graduated to a bus service. Flying fleas, we called them, probably because of the strange shape of their fronts with the driver's cab almost stuck on like an afterthought. Some of the first rides I recall are Sunday School treats to the seaside - treats indeed, and to be anticipated for weeks. I prayed every night, not to be ill for that day. And usually I wasn't. The bus couldn't get anywhere near to the Engine itself so we went to the nearest hard road to pick it up. What a buzzing beehive of children and parents there would be, some lucky enough to have bucket and spade clutched in hand from a previous year's visit or an elder brother's generosity. Such scrambling for the back seat, where although there was more chance of at least one of us being sick because of the bouncing, we could kneel up and wave at people as we passed them. Two thrills for the price of one. I remember one young lad being so excited that he had to have a wee in a seaside bucket held by his mother. They were sitting near the front. She rather unwisely opened the window and threw the contents of the bucket out, but the slipstream of the bus meant that it all flew in the back windows and splattered over us. Never mind, said various mothers, resignedly mopping us up and thinking that before we came home we'd be dirtier than that, what with sand and sea water all over our best clothes.

We thought, of course, that we would be at Hunstanton within minutes of starting, and it took all the concentration of the various parents on the bus to keep us looking forward. Just up the next bit ... just round the next corner. Wait till you smell the lavender fields at Heacham. Then you'll see the water tower at the top of the hill and you'll see the sea when we get up there. Honest. Now sit down and leave them sandwiches alone for the time being. And don't poke that spade in your sister's eye.

One girl who came to our Sunday School was so excited by the thought of her first outing that she worried about oversleeping. So she sat up all night on a chair beside her bed so as to be up early in the morning, then slept all the way to Hunstanton and missed most of the excitement.

CHILDHOOD DAYS AT STRETHAM, 1942 onwards

So, by a long and rather winding route, joined by many smaller pathways, this narrative reaches my own childhood.

Two sounds are tangled up in the front of my mind, caught in the sticky threads of memory and buzzing there like a bluebottle in a spider's web. Before they escape me, I must rush out and stab them into stillness. Like the spider, I have to feed on these memories if I am to go on to other times which are a little more certain in my mind. The two sounds are like and unalike; the buzz of a bee and the overhead grumble of a Lancaster bomber or some such great aircraft. It was my fourth birthday. I had been ill with influenza; had the doctor not managed to get his hands on some of the penicillin tablets just available after the war, I might not have survived. But by March of 1946 I was strong enough to sit outside in a little wooden chair, well wrapped in blankets, dazzled by the yellow crocuses that spread themselves wide to catch the hazy sunshine and welcome the first bees to sip their nectar. If I sat very still, a blue-tit would flit to the piece of cheese-rind suspended from a wire across the garden. The two house cats, Sam and Billy, were too well fed to bother and were stretched out on the blankets piled at my feet. The second sound, the aircraft – that was from Waterbeach Airfield, only a little distance across the fields from where we lived. They were still bringing troops and materials back from distant theatres of war. To this day the sound of a propeller-driven plane overhead brings back a ghost of a memory of that day, the child snatched from the brink of death to stare solemnly first down into the crocus cups and then up into the cloud-striped March sky.

The war itself had not affected me much, and I was only three years old when it ended. I believe that an RAF pilot who had to bale out and came knocking at our door was explained to me as Father Christmas, but I only recall being told, not the event itself, though he sat for a long time under my mother's eagle eye while father rang someone in the RAF to ensure that he wasn't a German in disguise. Father was thwarted in his desire to enlist; he was Reserve Occupation, engaged in keeping some kind of food production going in the days of the Atlantic Convoys and their losses. They made him a Heavy Rescue Air-Raid Warden, and he would tell of the night in the year I was born that, expecting invasion any moment, he and another warden were lying out on the river bank in the darkness and they heard a low swishing sound which they instantly recognized, from their training, as being a parachute. 'That's it, mate' father said. 'They're here!' They lay waiting as the sound increased, and passed over their heads. Only one parachute, and what was on the end of it was in fact an enormous landmine which got as far as the centre of Wilburton, the next village, before it detonated.

I was, of course, affected as were all children at that time by rationing. We had chickens, so there were always eggs, and our garden provided vegetables for us, but I was probably seven years old before I tasted butter. What we had until then was a block of something solid and vivid yellow called margarine. Mother would call it MMA – 'Margarine Masquerading As'. On the rare occasions when butter did come our way it was softened and mashed half and half into a block of this solid lump to make Half and Half. Tinned fish I could never face, though Mother often ate sardines on toast, or herrings in tomato. Sweets were rationed for a very long time. Father would buy one Mars bar and, slowly and carefully, cut it into slices, then we each took one slice at a time. The first potato crisps, made by Smiths, were very strange things – thick rather greasy slices of cooked potato, with salt in a little twist of blue paper. By the time I was eight or nine years old, the fish and chip wagon would come round and stop at the Cross in the middle of the village. One penn'orth of chips was quite exciting, shovelled into a cone of newspaper and most of it actually consisting of batter drips. And when the ice-cream van started to appear, that was another new sensation. All he had was large blocks of vanilla, of a strange primrose yellow colour. He would slice off a piece, slap it between two wafers and that was it.

There was a time when bread came off ration and sliced white loaves were available. They were considered almost like manna from heaven, because during the War bread had been made from any old flour combinations the bakers could get their hands on, half soya, sometimes with maize flour mixed in, and these new white loaves were a wonderful experience.

I never questioned the odd surrounding of my life. In fact, if a 100HP beam engine could have been considered a toy, that was how I saw it, the tall building giving me a special status because I was allowed to go to the top floor and could see all round me, whereas the other children from the farm were only permitted if I said so, and then one at a time. The Engine was surrounded by the Coal Yard, sheds, the carpenter's workshop which smelt enticingly of wood shavings and was presided over by Mr.Everitt, a dear old man with many skills to his hands who put up with my presence without complaint, so long as I was a good girl. There was the Diesel Engine, with all its mysterious valves and clicking machinery, and the cooling tank like some great swimming pool into which the water showered from a pipe when that Engine was running. To cross the main drain we used a walkway of planks called, most prosaically, 'The Boards' and a little further along was moored one of the two punts which were for reed-cutting but which I was allowed to use as soon as I could handle the 12ft lead-sheathed punt pole.

The district was divided into two parts, approximately one third to two-thirds, the greater area of land draining into the River Cam assisted by two great Allen diesels and the level of that part was lower than our end. So the trick was to take our punt down as far as the dam on main drain which divided the area, moor it up, climb over the dam and unloose the punt for the lower level which was waiting there, in which one had miles and miles of waterways to explore.

I spoke earlier of the keys having blocks of wood on them, in case they were dropped into one of the many waterways. Perhaps they should have put a block of wood on me, because long before I could swim, I managed to fall into all of them.

The day I fell into the river I was no more than five years old. I was playing with the other kids along the river bank, using sticks to push out into the main channel of the river the sheet ice which had broken away from the bank. Somehow I slipped and fell in. Did the other kids run and tell my parents – we were only just over the bank top from my house. No. They simply ran. And I was left floundering, clutching a handful of reeds in one hand and slowly feeling the numbing cold of that winter's afternoon soaking into me, taking away any wish to fight. I was crying out for help, but there was no-one around to hear me. One by one the fibres of the rushes began to part and my terror became torpor. Then over the wooden bridge came the grown-up cousin of some of my playmates, and he must have heard my screams because I am told he pedalled straight past their house, dropped his bike on the bank top and reached me before my remaining slender life-line finally broke away. So if Tony Badcock or any of his descendants in Stretham ever read this, may I put on record that I owe him my life.

Diana Cockrill

SKATING, FISHING AND OTHER DIVERSIONS

The river, the Old West which was the original course of the Great Ouse before Vermuyden intervened, played a great part in all our lives. Just as my mother had done, I skated, fished, swam and boated on, in and over it. Skating was usually January or early February. The waters would rise to flood the washlands and being only a few inches deep, would easily freeze. Sometimes the smaller drains such as the nine-foot would also freeze to bear, but we had to wait until either my father or Jack Day gave the word before we ventured onto that. During the winter of 1947 before the thaw that caused the floods, even the river froze for skating. It wasn't a case of white boots and silver blades, though, nor even of lethal ice-hockey skates. We used fen runners, which were kept tied in pairs in the shed during the summer. They were a blade of metal set into a cherrywood stock, and either turned up, or in a more decorative manner, curled over, at the ends. A long screw protruded in each heel, and leather straps threaded through the stock. One simply fastened the screw into one's boot heel and adjusted the straps. They were essentially a means of getting about rather than a recreational toy, those skates, descended from the Dutch habit of tying animal bones to their boots. One soon learned the art of pushing with the 'back' foot in order to force the 'front' foot to move, rather than trying to walk on the blades which just got you nowhere. Then you leaned into the wind and put your hands behind you, and took off. More than one clever-clogs I have seen with hands in pockets encountering a rough patch of ice where the reeds had made a hump and go head over heels. We had to be careful if we were on the washes, because the ice sloped down slightly towards the still liquid river, and it was all too easy to slip and slither down that path. If the river itself bore, a rare occasion, we were told never, never to go near the bridge, as the ice wouldn't bear under it, and to stay away from right-angled cracks.

Fishing was the next thing, as soon as the Close Season was over. We had to get our licence from Brunnings in Ely, though technically speaking we could have fished in the Main Engine Drain without one as it was an internal waterway and full of fish. Then came the excitement of getting our rods out, checking them, greasing the joints and running the line through the reel to make sure it still worked properly. Like my mother, I had accumulated a quantity of floats during riverside walks in winter, and pocket money permitted me to buy one or two more of my own. Lead shot, split so that we could slip the line into it and then bite it shut, just enough little roundels to keep the float bobbing upright. Hooks, of various gauges, either looped for tying or on their own length of gut or nylon. Eel hooks were very large and black. A disgorger to help get the hook out of a fish and a knife, in case it proved necessary to cut the trace because it had been swallowed hook and all. Then we were ready. Oh, and a rod rest too, and if we had the luxury of a keep net, a strong peg to hold it in place. The next question was bait. Stale bread, soaked in water, squeezed half dry by hand and finally twisted into a cloth, was the usual stuff. Rolling the paste in the meal of the chicken bin made it a little more appetising. Outside the back door was a place where mother always threw the tea-leaves, under the white rose bush, and it attracted big juicy worms which we dug and kept in a cocoa tin with a hole or two punched in the lid. Occasionally one of us would turn up with 'gentles', as we called maggots or blow-fly larvae, and no-one asked where they'd been found. When you live on a farm, there's very often a dead bird or rabbit lying around. I hated them, and wouldn't use them, but they did attract the fish.

What did we fish for? Bream, slender and silvery, were considered good enough if of a fair size to take home and eat. Roach and gudgeon would make our lives a misery, because they sucked at our worms, pulling the float under again and again, giving the impression that a much larger fish was on the hook. Perch we learned to handle with care, because he is a fighting fish, with a back fin of erectile spines which unless you gripped him tight would be enough to make you yell out in pain and drop him. I used to use my bait rag when I had a perch on the hook. Tench were mudfish, they never rose to our simple baits. But one summer evening, for some reason father had cause to pump our end of the district practically dry. I think, looking back, it was so that part of the Diesel pump could be examined that was normally under water, and I have vague memories of someone called Charlie actually going through the pump on a rope. What did amaze us all was the vast shoals of tench that were revealed. The Farm workers gathered on the sides of the waterway with pitchforks and sacks, heaving these huge fish out. Whether they were eaten or used as manure I don't know. Fishing for pike was a totally different game. To start with you used a deadline, an un-manned rod with an artificial bait at the end to which you had tied a live gudgeon to conceal the triple barbed hook. As you fished with your ordinary rod, you gave this deadline an occasional twitch with your foot to keep the spinner moving. If you struck, you knew it because even a small pike could almost tug the rod off the bank, and a big one was something for the older boys to deal with. You let out a yell of 'Pike. I'm got a pike!' and one of them would come running to help. I have seen a medium-size pike landed, and the young man who had done so shoved a pencil between its jaws, which closed with such force that the pencil was snapped in half. The Main Drain boasted several enormous pike that used to bask just below the surface of the water. Usually they'd slide off out of the way as the punt approached, but more than once I have hit one with the punt pole and the boat has tipped alarmingly as the great fish jack-knifed.

Swimming came next. I shall never know why it took me so long to learn to swim. We all played dangerously enough in the river during the summer. Garden Fete day at the end of June was usually the first day that parents, in general, gave permission to "go in the river" which in those days was clean enough. There was a shallow depression in which a dragline had bogged itself down years before, then a bed of fringed water lilies which marked the edge of the river bed itself. That was the bit you didn't go past until you could swim. As if such a constraint would have any effect on kids. We had old tractor inner tubes into which we threaded ourselves and thus held afloat we 'swam' across the river, up and down it too. I was only shamed into learning to swim when I went to Ely High School and had to try for the Beginners Width at the swimming gala in my first summer there. I learned by lying on my stomach on the gritty bed of the shallow depression, and dog-paddling my way off into deeper water, until in the end I found my buoyancy. And once across the river – well …

The washlands opposite the towing path were wide, a safety valve for the river when it rose, and the stretch opposite Engine House was rented to Harry Gotobed, rather an ogre to us children because he used to appear, or send his two sons Leslie and David, to clear us off his land. He didn't want the chance of gates being left open, cattle straying, but with the perversity of childhood we were forever trying to get on to Gutta's Wash, as we called it. Was he a goat in bed, or could the name have once been Goteberger, a true Viking name? Certainly his family was one of the oldest known in the village.

When we swam we used to haul out on to his washland and jump or dive back in, because on that side the deep water of the river's course was just below us. When a pleasure boat came up the river, we'd all haul out quickly on that side of the river, then someone would yell out 'Honeypot' and we'd jump in just as the boat passed, often with our hands linked under our bent knees so that we hit the water with our backsides, making one hell of a splash. But the main temptation was the hedge on the far side of Gutta's land, towering with hawthorn and willow, which in autumn was loaded with the biggest, juiciest blackberries you could wish for. Outwitting Gutta was our main aim. Looking back, if we'd gone to his house and asked him could we go and pick, I imagine he'd have given permission. He didn't want the blackberries himself.

My cousin and I both had rowing boats. Mine was clinker built. Father had bought it from the Keeper of Bottisham Locks, on the River Cam. It was painted green and cream, and was kept afloat under the bridge beside the scoop-wheel inlet, the flood gate having been concreted up in 1953. On a summer weekend, early in the morning I would collect my oars from the Boiler House, find the long ladder and drop it into the inlet, climb down it and untie my little craft. I'd paddle cautiously at first because it was not very deep and had mud banks, then once in the main stream of the river I was away. It was a different world, being between the edges of the river; even swimming wasn't the same because it was essentially a noisy, splashing sort of activity. But slipping along the river, with little curls of mist still rising, the smell of water mint and mud in my nostrils, I rowed past festoons of water forget-me-nots and beds of tall bulrushes, the real thing, not the reed-mace so often confused with them. Flowering rushes stood in elegant clusters and later in the summer the banks were patched with meadowsweet, like the cream on a coffee at the end of a good dinner, mixing with the scent of cut straw from the wheat fields and telling me clearly that the year had turned on its hinge again. I would see moorhens on their nests or with their broods of young, water voles scurrying about their housekeeping, sometimes a swan or a crested grebe. The former meant steering in towards the river edge and sitting still, because a roused cob could easily have upset my boat, especially if he had his pen and cygnets with him. The grebe were quite rare, fascinating because they would suddenly dive and vanish, only to pop up some distance away.

Rear View of Stretham Engine – left to right the house, the coal yard, Main Drain, the Engine and the Diesel Engine]

Going back to the days when I was younger, perhaps one Saturday morning in May father would say to me over breakfast 'They're shearing Main Drain today. Want to come and watch?' Did I! You may wonder about the word 'shearing', usually connected with sheep. Shearing, in the Fens, means clearing the water weed from a Main Drain, whereas roding is scything down the grass and weeds on its sides. Two of father's men would be waiting for him on The Boards, between them the massive chain-saw as wide as the Drain itself, with its polished handles. They would lift it over the boundary fences and then, making sure they have a good firm foothold on the sloping bank, would start to pull it across the Drain and back in a steady rhythm. The cut water weed would at first bob up in the air, then tumble sideways to lie on the surface, from which it was subsequently raked with a very long-handled rake and piled on the edges of thee fields so that the farmer could, if he chose, plough it in come October. I asked father one day why they spent time cutting all the water weeds down. He looked at me sideways, then decided to try and explain, and in fact it is a basic element of land drainage, so it will fit in at this point. Main Drain, which ended at the pumping engine, whether it was the Old Beam Engine herself or the Diesel that supplanted her, had to run at a downhill gradient so that the water would collect naturally. But if it was allowed to choke up with water weeds and lilies, the only time the water would move was when the engines were running. The rest of the time it would, strange as it may sound, start slowly to run back along the feeder drains and ditches until it was where it started from. That didn't please the farmers very much, especially if they were producing root crops which need steady irrigation but never to be soaked or they rot. In the larger section of the District, he explained to me, the dragline kept the Engine Drain, Division Drain and Railway Drain open at all times, but shearing was all they could usually manage at our end because getting the dragline up near us was quite, as he put it, a palaver involving a low-loader lorry, a tractor trailer borrowed from the farm, a supply of dam boards and a certain amount of heaving and swearing amongst the men detailed off to help..

When it did appear, it was a most exciting time. Wally Stern was its usual driver, just back from National Service and mostly wearing a stained old RAF beret. How and when his family came into the village I don't know, and of course I paid little attention to the troubles in Palestine, the outrages by the Stern gang. But looking back, Old Mr. Stern had a face that would have been at home at the Wailing Wall, his son Wally had thick black curls and some of the arrogance of the Jew, and the two Stern girls with their long blue-black hair could have stepped straight from Solomon's harem. Wally would sometimes let me climb up into the cab of the dragline while he ate his dockey. Obviously I couldn't be there when it was working. But if he dug up anything he thought would interest me, he would always climb down, pick it from the oozing dragline bucket and chuck it over to me. 'There y'are, what do yer make of that?' he'd ask with a grin.

There were other activities connected with the farming year. Sugar beet, if it survived the fen 'blows' of March and didn't end up in someone else's ditch or field, would have grown in long straight rows, but very thickly planted and needed systematic singling. First of all the farm men would go through the field, 'chopping out' with their hoes. They'd cut out a chunk of seedlings one hoe-blade's width, move on one width, chap out another, all down the rows. When that job was done, the women came in and from each little clump of seedlings would select the strongest, pulling up by hand all the others. It may seem a very wasteful method of cultivation, but the sugar beet that grew became enormous, having plenty of room to expand, whereas if they had not been singled they would have been no good. But it was back-breaking work, often conducted on hands and knees straddled over the rows of seedlings, the black dirt getting up your sleeves and into your nails so you ended up more like a coal-miner than a farm worker. It frequently coincided with the school Spring half-term, and we kids would be given a bit of land, perhaps an awkward corner where the women didn't want to work, to practice our skills on.

When I was very young the wheat was still harvested by cutter/binder, though it was tractor drawn. The sheaves would be tied by the machine and dropped off the end, and it was the job of the farm workers, the gang of women and, of course, us kids getting under every one's feet to prop them up in what we called shocks, I think it was eight sheaves, propped four against four, heads uppermost. The angle at which you propped them was critical – too wide, and simply placing the last one would cause the whole thing to tumble. It was possible to get inside one, but heaven help the child who managed to unbalance the structure! Going gleaning was traditional in September, a time-honoured custom. Once the cutter-binder had finished and the corn was stoked, or in later years the combine harvesters had quit the fields, we were allowed to go with our parents to gather up any spilt grain and ears of wheat. The grownups wore a gleaning apron, with the bottom turned up and stitched to make a sort of deep pocket, leaving both hands free to gather what had been spilt. There would be enough to feed the chickens for a large part of the winter by the time we'd finished, though we no longer made our own bread.

The main crop potato harvest took place during the October half term. Two kinds of machinery were used, the spinner and the hoover. The spinner had two giant circular sets of spikes, and they whirled round when it was drawn up the potato row, spinning the tubers out. It was less popular than the hoover, which left a neat row of exposed spuds. We children were allowed to help pick up the potatoes and put them into baskets which were thrown up into tractor trailers by the grown men. Our reward would be a big potato to take home at the end of the day. It kept us out of mischief, certainly.

With the first frosts it was time for the celery to be lifted. Fen celery is blanched by being earthed up in deep ridges. To harvest it, the whole plant is seized in one hand and jerked from the earth, not difficult as it is in fact not all that deep rooted, while the sharp cutting knife descends to swish off the main root. The celery is then neatly tossed in the air, reversed, and the top foliage is sliced off. It is work that needs a nimble hand and a keen eye. But there would be times when the knife would miss, or cut at a wrong angle, and then the whole plant would be slung to one side. These were the 'seconds' and it was permitted, within reason, to go down to the celery fields and help ourselves to a few roots. Nothing can be nicer than celery fresh from the earth, crisped by a good hard frost. The root would be cut into quarters and the excess soil washed off, and we'd eat it with slices of cheese and hot buttered toast made at the fire.

There is one other activity which is less pleasant to report – ratting. When the threshing tackle came along and the big wheat stacks were slowly dismantled, the mice and rats would huddle inside the base to the last minute. Word would go round that a stack was about to be finally pulled apart and it would be with glee that I'd grab a torch and one of the sticks from the shed, an ash pole or a blackthorn with a good big knob on the end, and join the others in the stackyard. As the circle of straw dropped lower and lower, someone would yell 'there they go' and we'd leap inside, trying to kill as many rats and mice as possible with our sticks. Bloodthirsty little monsters, perhaps, but it was all part of the natural cycle. To us it was as logical as a housewife wiping down the shelves in the cupboard before buying her winter supplies.

My mother speaks of getting skimmed milk from the farm along the bank. That was another way in which my young days resembled hers. Eddie, who was Polish, and either a POW or a refugee, memory fails me there, would milk down at Fidwell and Jack Day would fetch the churn up the drove to his house, where there was a cool dairy. Each family, earlier on that day, would have left at Jack's house their own milk can, with its lid, duly scalded clean, and however much milk we had ordered would be decanted direct into it. Sometimes the milk had cream an inch thick on the top. These cans would be stood on an old bench in their porch, in the deep shade, and it was up to us to go and fetch the milk home. I often exchanged this for helping wash up after Sunday lunch. During the summer we had to boil the milk so as it would not sour over night. We had no refrigerator, as there was no power. What did we do about the meat? The big walk-in pantry stood on the east side of the house, with only one window half of which was metal gauze so there was always a breeze coming in to keep the temperature down. The meat itself was delivered, by a butcher's boy on a bike with a huge square basket, on Saturday mornings. Some stewing steak, or in summer a pork pie, a big joint for Sunday, perhaps some sausages and some bacon. The joint would immediately be wiped over with vinegar, and perhaps a little salt rubbed into the bone if it was, say, leg of lamb or pork. Then all the meat was laid out, keeping each type separate, on a big flat dish, covered with a cloth and put in the meat safe, which stood on the tiled floor and had two doors, one of wire mesh and the other of yet more metal gauze. No way could flies get in through all that. The butcher would call again on a Tuesday, with supplies for the rest of the week. But it was very much a case of Stew on Saturday, roast on Sunday, cold on Monday with hot mashed potatoes and pickles and whatever was left was minced and made into shepherds pie for Tuesday. During the week, our main meal would be at 5.00 o'clock but at weekends we ate at lunch time [subject, as I have described, to father's appearing from the pub] and had tea at the end of the afternoon.

We had our little rituals. Sunday breakfast was always boiled eggs. Father had two. He could slice the top off his eggs with one cut of the knife, but I had to bang mine with the egg-spoon and then pick off the bits of shell. On Easter Sunday we would draw faces on the egg-shells and go out to hang them on the gooseberry bushes, to keep the witches away. Sliced bread hadn't been thought of then. The baker, too, came round with his wares in a big wicker basket. Mother would cut thick slices off the white loaf which made excellent 'soldiers' for dipping. Toast was reserved for winter, made with a toasting fork constructed out of twisted heavy-gauge wire. Father always carved the Sunday roast, but the top slice was put to one side and was mother's portion, though he served me, Nana and himself before he put it on her plate. She would be doling out the Yorkshire pudding, the vegetables and the gravy. Mother's speciality was a dark gingerbread, made with black treacle, which was served at tea-time.

SCHOOL DAYS AT STRETHAM

Although another World War had come and gone since my mother was at school, my memories of early days of education weren't all that different from hers. Stretham had changed only a little from the days when my father worked for Bert Parish as a 12-year-old boy whose job was to 'holler hold-ye', in other words to tell the cart horse when to move and when to stand still. Front Street had become High Street, Middle Street, to father's disgust, had been re-named Chapel Street and Back Lane was Read's Street, which he always maintained should have been Reed Street because of the large number of thatched houses there. The Village Pond had been drained, and the Mission Hall had gone – taken to Ely as some kind of meeting place, I believe. So Hall Corner was now called Sun Corner, and Pond Street was Newmarket Road. But Pump Lane was the same, Cage Lane too. It differed from mother's village of Pymore in that it did have two schools, and they were in the village, but each of them had only two large rooms for teaching, and in each room there were two classes doing separate things at the same time, except when, at the Primary School, we listened to Broadcasts for Schools.

I've mentioned Mrs. Vail who lived next door to us, in the Stokers Cottage. She was responsible for my very dramatic start at the Infants School. I imagine she meant no harm, but when my fifth birthday came round, and then the date for my starting school in the summer term, she chanced to see me on the previous day and said it was my last day of freedom. So, when I was finally taken up to the village on the little child seat fixed to the inner frame of mother's bike and deposited outside the Infants School with instructions to go through the gate, I simply clung to the railings and screamed defiance. Nothing my mother or any of the other mothers around could do or say would detach me. I don't know what I was imagining or why I was so terrified, but in the end the very prosaic Infant Teacher, Miss Kitson, simply came through the gate, took my hands off the railings and said 'Come along, Diana, time to come in now' and I did. Perhaps I recognised Authority, with a capital 'A', even then. I have few memories of being at the Infants School. I know that on the corner of the patch of land which had once been the village pond there was a row of rather dilapidated cottages in one of which lived an elderly lady who used to like to wave at us children as we walked primly up into the back gate. We decided, helped along by a comment from her grandson who was at the 'Top School', that she was a witch and used to scream and run if she came out into the yard. It was a good thing that she was deaf, or she might have been very upset.

My mother talks of walking everywhere. I took it for granted that our transport would be bikes. Almost everyone in the village rode one. I started early on a three-wheeler red trike. But there was no way I would be able to ride the mile separating us from the village, so my mother, bless her, tied a rope to the handlebars of the trike, told me to put my feet in the bend of the frame and leave the pedals to whiz round, and then mounting her own bike she towed me up Green End Road. As soon as possible I learned to ride a two-wheeler and before I was seven years old I was making the journey twice a day. It should have made me healthy, but all it did was give me huge calf muscles. So much for the claims of the medics!

One thing I have to admit still makes me cringe with shame. Until I went to school I had not used a knife and fork, but been content with what was known as a 'spoon and pusher' set given me as a christening present. So when, in due course, a canteen was built for the Infants and school dinners were organised, I was in a real dilemma and Miss Kitson enquired whether it was because I didn't like the food that I was dropping so much of it on the floor!

They tried to teach me to knit, but it was not a success. By the time I had laboriously managed a length of what was politely called 'a scarf for your dolly', children in the class below mine had made entire layettes for theirs. But I took to reading quite eagerly, and it wasn't long before I'd discovered the art of reading without saying the words out loud. After that nothing in the bookshelves was safe from me, though I didn't understand half what I read. I remember enjoying the Little Grey Rabbit stories of Alison Utley, and another series about Sam Pig and Brock the Badger, but after one or two books like father's copy of The Decameron had been put under lock and key, I was allowed to roam where I wished in the bookshelves. Father and mother were well-read, and would often quote snippets of poetry to one another. I was familiar with Rupert Brooke's 'Granchester' by the time I was seven years old, never dreaming that it was only a few miles up the road. And Kipling was easy enough to learn, with his fine robust metre and steady rhymes.

They also between them taught me to sing. Father had an excellent tenor voice, and though he could not read music he easily learned anything that mother played through for him on the piano. He used to sing to me when I was in bed, to send me to sleep, cowboy songs like Home on the Range, and Old Faithful, and at village entertainments he would dampen many an eye with his rendition of Mother Machree or Galway Bay. In fact, riding round the District in his jeep, if I was inside the cab with him, we would happily raise our voices in Lily Marlene or Goodbye, Dolly Gray. I sang in my first concert when I was seven; Stainer's 'Crucifixion' in the Parish Church. Needs must – mother was playing the organ and father was singing one of the tenor solos, and that was in the days before grandmother Linda came to live with us. If you know the work you will also know that it is interspersed with hymns for the congregation to sing, and very wisely mother taught me the tunes of them, but forbade me to join in anything else though I was to stand with the grown-ups.

So two years passed at the Infants School, and when I was seven years old I 'went up' to 'the Top School' as the Primary was known, probably because it was up a slight rise. It, too, had only two rooms, each heated by a huge round tortoise stove. There was no question in my early days of free milk for us children, nor were there any facilities for a midday meal. We brought our own sandwiches if we lived out of the village, and the desks were turned back to back, with a sheet of oil-cloth [vinyl you would call it today] laid over them to form a makeshift table. Dried powdered milk was provided, but it had to be mixed with cold tapwater and was very unpleasant, with lumps of powder that burst in your mouth. Even when free milk finally arrived, it was left outside the school very early in the morning in a crate, and often was frozen solid. So the whole crate would go inside next to one of the stoves, where it swiftly became luke-warm. My cousin says it put her off hot milk for life.

The Head Teacher was Mr. Poole, a fiercely erudite man with a strong sense of discipline. His second in command was Mr. Blackmore who also thought nothing of laying a ruler across the palm of any disobedient child. The school was old, and had a bell-tower, though there was no longer a bell in it to ring us to classes. The upper playground was for the boys only, just as well as it was where their toilet was, a very primitive affair with a tar-paper backing and a gutter with a drain at the end. The boys would play a game of their own, called stingy, involving a hard leather ball flung at the ankles of fleeing friends. The only time we girls were allowed in there was if it froze, when the caretaker would sling a bucket of water from top to bottom of the playground two or three times, thus making an excellent slide. If you went down it fast, you ended up tumbling straight into the side cloakroom. In the main playground there was also a ritual game called 'Wall to Wall' with one catcher in the middle of the playground, and groups of us trying to run from one end to the other without being 'tagged'. The boundary wall of the school had some sections that were flat on top and some that were peaked, like a shed roof. You judged your ability by how soon after arrival at Top School you learned to walk along the length of the wall without either falling or having to jump off.

In the playground was a huge plane tree, and each autumn it produced its seeds, chains of bobbles which disintegrated if squeezed. The trick was to crush one of these bobbles and then push the pieces down the back of someone's shirt or jumper, where they lodged between the shoulder blades and itched dreadfully all day.

It was there that I learned to skip through the long rope turned by two big girls. We used to chant

All the boys on the bank lead a merry life
Except ****** and he needs a wife.
A wife he shall have, and a'courtin he shall go
Along of ****** 'cos he loves her so.
Two, four, six, eight – who do we appreciate?

And we'd yell out the name of one of the most popular boys, to his intense confusion.

When I first 'went up' that there were several boys in their mid teens still in school, because no secondary education had been found for them. Later, one or two would go to the Cromwell School at Wisbech, and by the time I took the 11-plus, there was a secondary modern school on the old airfield at Witchford. One of the boys in my class had a very stout mother, rather more pugnacious than usual and blessed with three sons all of whom were 'young varmints' and up to mischief all day long. She would come steaming up to the school and could be heard all over the building saying 'My ***** in't done no wrong'. The Head Teacher used to vanish when he heard her voice.

Our school was a Church of England foundation, which meant two additional days off. The first one was Ash Wednesday, but we all had to go to church in the morning, parading two and two across the road where we were joined by a crocodile of infants all in their smartest outfits. I had a secret which I shared with no-one else but my father – deep in his Waterbeach area was an old house with a garden which, by Ash Wednesday, would be drifted over with great clumps of snowdrops, and he would pick me up in the jeep after the service and take me out there, as he always had some reason to go into Waterbeach Fen. I never picked any, just sat and stared at their beauty. One day the old lady who lived there came out and saw me, but she didn't scold, so I think father must have asked her permission before he ever took me there. The other day was Ascension Day, which of course moved up and down the calendar depending on the date of Easter. Again, we had to be at church, and anyone who tried bunking off would soon hear about it. We had a hearty respect for the Attendance Officer, Mr. Clough and always shot to our feet if he came into the classroom. There was merit to be gained by having a good attendance record, because one other benefit of being a Church School was Attendance Money. It was a very formal process, with the school governors in a semi-circle at one end of the room and each pupil entering in order of the amount they had 'earned' by good attendance. The money came from Mrs. Martha Digby's charity, which required, according to a notebook belonging to one of my Sennitt ancestors, by Will dated February 11th 1716, her Trustees 'yearly and every year for ever six days before Easter and six days before Christmas to pay unto six of the poorest widows of Stretham a sum of money.' In 1913 when the notebook was written this was seven shillings and sixpence. After the widows had been paid, coal and clothing were purchased for the needy. In 1913 there were about 146 recipients of this hand-out. Finally a sum [in 1913 £25] was allotted to the scholars of Stretham school for regular attendance. One year a great furore broke out because the school governors decided in their wisdom to give out books telling of significant events in the life of Jesus instead of the money. I imagine that things subsequently became difficult for them, because the following year we were back to money.

Then came the 11-plus, the Scholarship which, if passed, guaranteed us a place at either Ely High School if we were girls or Soham Grammar School for the boys. Children were promised a new bike, or a week by the seaside, if they did well. I knew that I was one of the cleverest children in the class, with the exception of arithmetic, 'sums' as we called it. Mental arithmetic I could cope with, though. Writing and spelling were a cinch. Once we had a spelling 'bee' involving the whole school. It started with words of three letters like *cat* or *dog* and once you reached a word you couldn't spell, you put your pencil down and stopped. I kept going, and kept going, aware after some time that I was the only one writing and had probably been so for a long time. But they had to go on until I foundered on something. Bear in mind that I was only 10½, but we had been taught to spell by syllables and it was that which finally defeated me. 'Assassinate' I almost got, but actually wrote 'assinate' and seeing me hesitate Mr. Poole said, with some relief, 'Well done' and declared the contest over. I think it was some kind of national test we had taken part in, and my spelling age was given as that of a 15-year old, but I am not certain.

There were three attempts at the 11-plus in those days. If you passed first time you had a place in the A-stream of the secondary school. A pass at the second attempt meant going into the Alpha, and if you had almost reached the desired standard but not quite, you had to go for an interview with examples of your work, which might persuade the Education Authority to let you into the Remove. There was always the chance, of course, to be promoted, or sent down, a level. I was eating my tea on the day after I'd taken the exam when father came in. 'I saw Mr. Bayliss' he said to mother. I knew the man he talked of, one of the school governors. 'He said she was going to be all right.' I remember they smiled at one another.

So began the final parallel with my mother's life, my time at Ely High School. It was very different from her days there, though for my first four years I was in the same building, Bedford House in Ely. Like her, I still had a cycle journey but mine was much shorter, just the mile each way. I'd leave my bike at Grandma's, and then after she went into Tower House home in Ely, I left it with an older girl called Betty who lived at the top of Green End Road. From the village we went on the bus. We High School girls, very conscious of our smart uniforms, gathered at what was then the bus stop outside The Chequers pub and caught the 109 bus at 8.40 a.m. The 'Witchford lot' – those who had failed the scholarship – waited on the other side of the road by the Post Office for their own private hire bus, a green single decker. We had to wear our berets on the bus – navy to start with, then yellow as you became a prefect. The boys who went to Soham Grammar School had long since departed on their own bus that went cross-country. There were one or two boys, rather cissies we thought them, who attended the Kings School in Ely. They were paid for, and the general impression was that they wouldn't have passed the scholarship had they taken it, but they'd probably been at some kind of Prep School and not had to bother. 'Horrid little tykes' we used to call them. And three girls, quite clearly higher mortals than we would ever be, went off on the early bus to Cambridge as they were enrolled at The Perse School. As they were respectively the daughters of the Butcher, the Grocer and the Head Teacher, that caused a certain amount of mirth.

My days at the High School were very much the same as those of any fairly clever girl in the 1950's, some parts to be enjoyed, some to be loathed. It was there that I became aware of my skill with languages, becoming fluent in French and learning creditable German. I learned to bake cakes, and decorate them, to avoid playing hockey, to write poetry, to sew my own clothes. I had crushes on some of the prefects, then became one myself. We moved school to a special new building on Downham Road, and in the sixth form I was one of a group who advertised it for sale in the local paper and pasted up the slogan 'Abandon Hope, all ye who enter Here' on all the entrance doors on the eve of one April Fools Day. Out of courtesy, the one over the staff entrance was in the original language, 'Lasciate ogni speranza, voi ch'entrate' which mitigated our scolding by the Head Teacher, herself a classics scholar. It wasn't 'in a moment, in the twinkling of an eye, at the last trumpet' that I was changed, but I think that going to High School was for both my mother and myself the beginning of the end.

Yet not so. By the time I was in my middle teens, father was earning enough – though it was still pitifully small by most standards – to allow us to go on holidays, staying at what were called Christian Endeavour Holiday Homes. Troon, on the Firth of Clyde, Conway in North Wales. Always travelling by train. And I would notice that as we came south, or east, once we passed Peterborough or March both father and mother would seem to relax a little. I didn't question why at that time, but now, if ever I visit Wisbech, or Ely, or Cambridge, as soon as the train begins to pull out across Waterbeach Fen, or the coach crosses the Nene at Guyhirn and the black soil, dropped below the road embankment, is revealed, the horizon lightens from edge to edge and the reeds sigh in the ditches, or I catch from the A10 a first glimpse of the white roof of 'my' cathedral, something in me, something of what my parents were feeling, something which will last as long as I do, gives a little contented sigh and whispers 'Home'.

So let there be a conclusion, something written when, many years later, I studied at University for an Honours degree in English and French. Although what follows bears another title, it could as well be called Parallels as not, and is perhaps the best final tribute to my mother, my father, and our days as dwellers in the Black Fens.

DARK PASTORAL

Time and the hand of man
Have greatly changed this land of sky and water.
Black soil which once beneath salt floods lay low
Now billows between banks in mad March blow.
The high-raised rivers gleam like stainless steel
Across whose surface sunset splendours wheel
Torching the lesser clouds, so the whole air
Throbs deep with red and gold, pale only where
Soft pink and amber hold the sky in thrall.
A descant to the evening's minor, dying fall.

Remote, unfashionable,
They have a beauty of their own, these fens.
Wide acres turning with the passing year
From black to green, and then with wheat in ear
From edge to edge each field a golden sigh
Replete with harvest; on the drove nearby
Blood-burst of poppy stains the silverweed.
Deep in the ditch among the clustered reed
A warbler boils and bubbles in the sun.
And Colin Clout rejoices, for his work is done.

No shepherd he.
Sheep do not flourish on these marshy meads.
Yet he has guardian duties to perform.
When frost and snow grip hard, then thaw to storm
His flock, the banks - his fold the level land.
See where on watch he climbs, lantern in hand
Deep in the sullen hours of windy night
Checking by gauge-board mark the water's height.
Then down, boots slithering in the blue gault clay
To prime and run his engine for another day.

Diana Cockrill

Now raise your chimmney'd head
You who were built to serve this threatened sward
It is your task the deluge to contain
Though nature serves you ill with gale and rain.
Whilst sweating churls with coal your boilers fire
Creating steam to thrust your piston higher.
Your cast iron beam lifts up alternate ends
Con-rod to fly wheel swift the message sends.
The sluice-gate opens, pushing 'gainst the tides
And water surges twixt the inlet's muddy sides.

Thus Colin strives to win.
With culverts blocked and sandbag barriers built
The wolf is kept outside the sheepfold gate
Until with opened sluice the floods abate.
Then crocus cups the gardens scarf with gold
And joys of Spring his cottage home enfold.
The crown imperial lifts its drooping bells
While Phyllis to their child the legend tells.
White-clad above the lawn the plum tree blows
Foretelling summer with the budding China Rose.

Oft in the evening hush
Colin and Phyllis in their garden strive
With hoe and rake tending the fertile soil,
Setting high cloches, later frosts to foil,
Where cats will bask if carelessness permits
And on whose ridge the thwarted sparrow sits.
On Sabbath eve upon the bridge he'll stand
The shepherd and redeemer of the land.
Yet homeward bound, ne'er fails to raise his eye
To read on engine wall this motto written high:

These fens have oft times been by water drowned
Till science a remedy in water found.
The power of steam, she said, shall be employed
And the destroyer by itself destroyed.